COURAGE, CHURCH!

COURAGE, CHURCH!

Essays in Ecclesial Spirituality

Walbert Bühlmann

Translated by Mary Smith

ORBIS BOOKS

Maryknoll, New York 10545

1978

The Catholic Foreign Mission Society of America (Maryknoll) recruits and trains people for overseas missionary service. Through Orbis Books Maryknoll aims to foster the international dialogue that is essential to mission. The books published, however, reflect the opinions of their authors and are not meant to represent the official position of the Society.

First published as *Coraggio, Chiesa!* by Edizioni Paoline, Rome, 1977, copyright © by Walbert Bühlmann

This translation copyright © 1977 by St. Paul Publications, Slough SL3 6BT England

U.S. edition, 1978, by Orbis Books, Maryknoll, NY 10545

Nihil obstat: D. A. Valente ssp
Imprimatur: F. Diamond vg, Northampton

This edition typeset in Great Britain and printed in the United States of America

Library of Congress Cataloging in Publication Data

Bühlmann, Walbert.
  Courage, church!

  Translation of Coraggio, chiesa!
  Bibliography: p.
  1. Church—Addresses, essays, lectures. 2. Mission of the Church—Addresses, essays, lectures. 3. Spiritual life—Catholic authors—Addresses, essays, lectures. I. Title.
BX1746.B8313 1978   262'.001   78-1381
ISBN 0-88344-068-7

CONTENTS

ABBREVIATIONS

AAS   Acta Apostolicae Sedis, Vatican.

AG   Ad Gentes. Conciliar Decree on the Church's Missionary Activity.

GS   Gaudium et Spes. Conciliar Pastoral Constitution on the Church in the world of today.

LG   Lumen Gentium. Conciliar Dogmatic Constitution on the Church.

LThK   Lexicon für Theologie und Kirche, Freiburg.

NZM   Neue Zeitschrift für Missionswissenschaft, Schöneck.

PC   Perfectae Caritatis. Conciliar Decree on the renewal of the religious life.

PMV   Pro Mundi Vita, Brussels.

SC   Sacrosanctum Concilium. Conciliar Constitution on the Liturgy.

INTRODUCTION

After too long a period during which theology remained
static and abstract, there is now a return to the dynamic
theology of the Fathers and the Bible, and thus to the idea
that God's self-revelation — as the God who is always
close to his people, consoling them and encouraging them
through thick and thin — is to be found less in doctrinal
propositions than in historical events. Biblical exegesis has
gradually come to favour greater stress on God's loving
care for his people of old, and this same theme underlies
the new approach to theology as a whole.[1]

But a question at once arises. Are we simply to take
a look backwards in time, as when visiting a museum, and
gaze at things which belong to the past and have no place
in the present? If that were indeed the case we might
perhaps find it all quite interesting but rather beside the
point. For nowadays man is concerned far less with past
history than with history in the making, his own present
history; he wants to know how he ought to live through
and evaluate current events, and whether there is any
profound meaning lying hidden behind so many happenings
which on the face of it are meaningless and even absurd.
As he sees it, the question can be expressed in the form
of blunt alternatives: either salvation history has carried
on right up until the present day or there is no such thing
as salvation history; either every people is a chosen people
or there is no chosen people at all. Now, God is completely

impartial and certainly has no favourites (Rm 2:11). Thus the history of salvation in ancient times can carry weight as a very strong case in point but it cannot be deemed the one and only case. Salvation history certainly did not begin with Abraham and end with Christ; it has gone on since Christ right up until Paul VI, and it will go on for as long as there is a Pope occupying the See of Peter. We must not forget the prophecy of Malachi.

Given all this, surely no member of the Church can ever succumb to fear and take refuge in timidity — even when some developments are far from welcome, even if Yahweh should blaze with anger against his people, as expressed anthropomorphically in the Old Testament (Ex 32:11; Ps 7:12; Is 47:6, etc.), even if Jesus should choose to sleep while a storm threatens the boat, as expressed in more human and christian fashion in the New Testament (Mt 8:24), even if a few age-old church institutions and structures are subjected to attack by younger elements convinced that the wine of the Gospel is always new and still fermenting and must therefore always be poured into new skins, not only in Christ's own day but in every age.

In none of these circumstances should the Church, being what she is, ever echo the moans of the inveterate malcontents or indulge in the hesitancy of the fainthearts. She must move forward courageously herself and imbue the whole of humanity with confidence in the future. It was for this, and for this alone, that Christ established her in this world. Her purpose is to proclaim the good news, spread hope and radiate courage, secure in the knowledge that the Lord remains true to his promises. And the Church is not someone unidentified living somewhere unspecified. We ourselves are the Church.

The following pages reproduce the texts of some lectures and articles of mine dating from 1975 and 1976. Publication of my book *The Coming of the Third Church*[2] brought me many invitations from Europe and elsewhere to expand and go more deeply into various points raised in that volume. I now realise that all through these essays I have pursued and developed — though without consciously intending to — one lead idea: that salvation history is still in the making here and now, for us and through us, and that we must therefore press on, without wavering or faltering and with heads held high, through everything and despite everything. I permit myself the hope that this little book may prove of service to the Church at this present time.

Walbert Bühlmann, O.F.M. Cap.

I

THE RESURRECTION OF JESUS
AND THE FUTURE OF THE CHURCH

To look backwards in history to the resurrection of
Jesus is certainly indispensable, for the resurrection laid
the unshakeable foundations of our faith. But if our look
backwards is not to leave us bogged-down in sterile theological debate it must at the same time be a look forwards:
the resurrection must always lie ahead on the horizon
for the pilgrim Church, influencing the whole of the
Church's life throughout history, no less now than in
earlier centuries. The accounts of the resurrection must
not suffer the fate of so many fine conciliar and post-
conciliar texts and remain, alas, nothing but fine words.

Nowadays there is abundant talk of crisis in the
Church and of a dark future ahead for her. We are certainly experiencing a large-scale exodus, avowed and
unavowed, from membership of the Church. Secularisation
threatens not only to set religion free from myths that are
no longer credible but also to set man free from religion
itself. In a number of countries the Church is in a delicate
situation politically and has to endure restrictions placed
on her freedom of action; in others, by contrast, ecclesiastical circles are reacting to the irresistible social changes
of our time with defeatism and panic fear. In such circumstances it is preferable to rely on the principle for-
mulated by Pastor in his *History of the Popes* — that

11

the Church's periods of deepest humiliation are always the periods of her greatest strength, and that death and the tomb are not signs of her end but symbols of her resurrection.[1]

History, however, provides no 'proof' that the Church has a future. The fact that her past goes back two thousand years does not guarantee her a further two thousand. Belief in the Church's future rests on faith alone, on contemplation of the risen Christ.

I. The resurrection of Jesus is the formal principle, the raison d'être, of the Church's existence past, present and future

But for Easter, all would have been over. The disciples going to Emmaus would have lost all hope (Lk 24:21). There would probably have been further prophets, further messiahs — and further disillusionment.

But Christ rose, and by his resurrection has shown himself to be the full realisation of all man's hopes and transcendental aspirations. He is 'man-made-perfect' because he is 'God-made-man'. And he has given us hope in an absolute future.

Christ, the one who died and rose again, is God's investment in human history. The resurrection of Jesus is God's decisive eschatological act, God's self-revelation in advance: for the resurrection clearly demonstrates who God is — the one whose power extends over life and death, whose integrity and fidelity remain unimpaired no matter what catastrophes befall. Easter means that the limitations of this finite world have been overcome. For the Christian there is always room in life for God's interventions — his surprises, his freshly creative potential. The destiny of the whole world hinges on the resurrection of Jesus. Thus the resurrection-faith is not merely one truth alongside many other truths: it sums up and underpins the entire christian faith. With it stand or fall belief

12

in Christ and belief in God; with it stand or fall the past, present and future of the Church. Whoever denies the one denies the others. And vice versa: those who fear for the future of the Church implicitly deny the resurrection of Jesus.[2]

But Christ raised from the dead is our faith (1 Cor 15:20). He died once for all and will never die again (Rm 6:10). Hence his Church cannot fail to have a future.

II. What this truth means in practice

1) The Church has an existence that is permanent and timeless

This follows immediately from what has already been said. The risen Christ is the invisible but nonetheless real pivot on whom human history will turn until the *parousia*. Easter and the *parousia* are not simply two events beginning and ending the christian era; they are two magnetic poles, each exerting a balanced pull throughout the duration of the christian era. The Church, by contrast, is the visible sign of Christ's presence, the tool he uses.

We have here two truths of 'faith'. Only by meditating on the events of Easter is it possible to discern the divine Christ in the human, historical figure of Jesus, and to welcome him with a lifelong vote of confidence in him. 'Low' christology (the Christ of history) and 'high' christology (the Christ of dogma) do not contradict one another but are complementary. Similarly with ecclesiology. 'Low' ecclesiology, with its emphasis on the Church of phenomenology and concrete experience, can sometimes be disconcerting. But 'high' ecclesiology reassures us that in spite of her all-too-human appearance the Church is a divine mystery (LG 1), worthy not only of study but of meditation.

That the Easter faith can inspire boundless and unshakeable confidence has been amply demonstrated by the apostles and martyrs, confessors and religious of earlier

13

times. Today however — "and it is with tears that I say it" (Ph 3:18) — maoist-inspired movements outdo us in commitment as well as in confidence that their beliefs can change the world for the better.. So we must recover the dynamic thrust of christianity inspired by the fact that the Church exists timelessly, permanently.

Yet the Church does not exist a-temporally or supra-temporally; quite the reverse:

2) The Church has an existence within history

If the Church had no role to play in history, there would have been no need to found her: the glorified Christ himself would have more than sufficed. But he, on stepping out of what the historians call history, entrusted his Church with the task of being the visible sign of the mystery of his presence within history.

So the Church, the people of God, does not live apart from history but forms part and parcel of it, acting as leaven and yeast within it.

History is made up of progress, movement, change, struggle, suffering, hope. The image of the 'Rock of Peter', immutable in the face of every storm, has often given rise to mistaken attitudes of mind: "The Church has plenty of time! The Church is eternal! She should not try to keep pace with hurried modern trends, for these will die a natural death whereas the Church will live on . . .".

But God is the God of the living, not of the dead; he is the God of a history that is always in the making from minute to minute, not merely the history of past ages but the history of every 'today'.

The Church is accused of often giving facile answers, 'eternal' answers pre-fabricated centuries ago to fit each and every case. Answers of this kind no longer make any impression. The genuine questions now being asked by present-day man are prompted by suffering and real-life experience. So, genuine answers will be forthcoming only

14

if there is participation, com-prehension, com-passion. "We need to plunge with courage and simplicity into situations as they arise. One saves oneself not by standing still on 'the shores of eternity' only to get swept off one's feet and drowned by the tide of time, but by swimming boldly out and moving with that tide".[3]

If the Church lacks the courage to tread the paths cut by history and adapt herself to new realities, extending a welcome to movements like those set in train by St Francis of Assisi and John XXIII, other forces will come along and do what needs to be done, movements like those of Robespierre, Garibaldi, Mao. History shapes its own course; and if we decline to change ourselves, change itself will change us.

3) The Church's existence is ensured by God

Although the Church must live and move forward with and within history, the fundamental reason for her existence and her future is something, or rather someone, beyond history: the risen Christ. So the Church's future is qualitatively different from the futures of all earthly kingdoms and nation-states, which seek self-perpetuation by human means.

But Christ has not yet brought into play, within history as we know it, all the effective signs of his power; he has not yet manifested the glory of his 'basileia'.

So the Church's future will not be exempt from catastrophe: indeed it is bound to include catastrophes of all kinds; but amid them all the Church will perceive, as she experiences the dark night, that salvation and her own future are God's prerogative.[4] The clarion call of Easter Day does not blot out the mourning lament of Good Friday. He who is risen is he who underwent crucifixion; and the Church to come, when history is complete, the Church of the resurrection, will be the Church that has undergone crucifixion.

Throughout history the Church has been and will

be tempted to ensure her continuing existence and her future by human means, depending for security on guarantees and concordats and on financial and political power. But this turns her into a purely human affair, an 'establishment', a 'bourgeoisie', as her history since Constantine amply demonstrates. We are at present making the final effort to shake ourselves free of the medieval conviction that the Church must be powerful. In the document on religious freedom, the second Vatican Council enunciated the theological basis for the right approach. From now on our message will be offered, not imposed, freely accepted or equally freely rejected. In many countries both old and young, people are reacting strongly against a Church which used to be powerful. Laicist elements want to go their own way, totally independent of all Church 'aid' and 'works'. Perhaps this is the hour of grace in which the Church is being reshaped and recommissioned for her specific function — to be for the world the sign of hope and love.

4) *The Church exists to fulfil a mission to the world*

The Church does not exist for her own sake, to live in 'ecclesiocentrism'. On the contrary: she must count for less and less in her own eyes and live only for the sake of others — for the world, for the whole of humanity.

The risen Christ is the guarantee of all salvation. He took upon himself the misery of the human condition and overcame it. Ever since, he has been the invisible dynamic thrust behind every effort to achieve what is good. The resurrection of Jesus, after his condemnation and execution, guarantees that there is no misfortune, no desperate situation that cannot be mastered thanks to the faithfulness and the creative power of God. His is the strength that will open the graves dug by darkness and despair.

This hope, albeit eschatological, is operative already in our own time. It spurs us to step out boldly towards

16

the 'promised land', to break the vicious circles created by ignorance and disease, poverty and violence, and all that makes no sense in life. The Christian cannot remain apathetic, lethargic or indifferent but must set about building a world of reconciliation and salvation. Whenever we give food to the hungry or work to the workless, whenever we restore dignity to the shamefaced or freedom to the oppressed, whenever we grant forgiveness to a sinner or give fresh hope to one in despair, we enact Easter, in that we get the better of a situation devoid of hope. The Easter event thus becomes a thoroughly up-to-date reality and not a fine story of once-upon-a-time — a reality that will stay up-to-date until the *parousia*. And we are present all over again as our Lord and Saviour passes on his way.

Those actions then become, analogously, 'sacramental signs'; for they give us live experience of God present and active in human history.[5]

The specific service which the Church has to render to the world has nothing to do with technical advice, masterly pronouncements, generous 'aid' hand-outs. Her *idée fixe* should be the idea of hope. Her basic state of mind should be one of confident trust. Her task is to radiate light where there is darkness, to speak words of hope where there is despair, to inject fresh courage into hearts that are dispirited, and thus to preach salvation to all men.

Within such a perspective there is no danger of the Church's mission going through a crisis or being brought abruptly to an end. Far from it: we are at the beginning of a new and quite extraordinary missionary era. So long as men inhabit the earth they will always need hope and will always seek a meaning to life. The animals have no such problems; they are guided by their instinct. Primitive man had comparatively few problems, for he followed unquestioningly the traditions and customs of his tribe. But modern man (and he is to be found everywhere today) has demolished the traditional systems which gave

17

him security and now exists in a void with regard to all the fundamental problems of life. He is back where man started and is therefore, more than ever before, groping in search of what he lacks. So anyone with good news to impart to him has every chance of making its impact felt.

Moreover, that Christ is risen is a perennially valid fact that no amount of history will ever be able to annul. We must therefore go on proclaiming the risen Christ, who is the principle of the Church's hope for the present-day world.

II

ELEMENTS OF A FRESH ECCLESIOLOGY

It is nowadays fairly generally held that although the so-called 'primitive' peoples lead a life that technically speaking is very poor, they nonetheless preserve a sound and balanced outlook and feel in no way insecure within the framework of their own concept of the world, whereas modern man is making scarcely believable progress in matters technical — and feels very sure of himself in this respect — but nonetheless remains full of doubts over the decisive questions life poses. This spiritual disorientation is something that even priests and religious fall prey to; more and more of them are becoming uncertain about their role and identity within the Church.

Until about twenty years ago we were the proud possessors of an ecclesial theology that was soundly structured and unassailable. It was of course a somewhat poverty-stricken theology, but this was perceived by only a few enlightened spirits. If we examine the classic textbook by A. Tanquerey,[1] used in many European seminaries for decades on end, we find that in his treatise on the Church he devotes sixty-four pages, under four main headings, to proving that Christ founded the Church (a) as an infallible authority, (b) as a perfect society, (c) as a hierarchic society and (d) as a monarchic society. In a further small section of a mere couple of pages he adds that the Church is the Body of Christ and the Bride of Christ. This concept of the Church as a pyramidal

19

structure remained in force until just before the second Vatican Council; in fact the *schema* on the Church drawn up by the preparatory theological commission still followed this line exactly.

Then, set in motion by the Holy Spirit and accelerated by pressure from the better bishops and their theologians, the new pentecostal wind came rushing in. Suddenly we had the great joy of rediscovering the Church for what she really is. The thoroughgoing Dogmatic Constitution *Lumen Gentium* begins by presenting the Church as a mystery, as the original sacrament of salvation, as the consoling presence of God within human history. Its second chapter describes the Church as the people of God, and relates charismatic gifts and the priesthood of all believers to this theme. Finally the third chapter speaks of the hierarchy as called to serve the people of God. So we have gone back to the ways of thought of the first three centuries — centuries which must always remain normative because the Church was then indeed experienced as mystery, whereas after Constantine she developed more and more the characteristics of an empire.

Let me now try to say a little more about this new — or, rather, very old — ecclesiology. A very beautiful model for comparison comes to mind: the architecture of St Peter's. The first thing to make an overwhelming impression on the crowds of pilgrims entering this is the great yellow window of the apse, with its dove representing the Holy Spirit; in the afternoon especially, and towards sunset, the enormous interior is flooded with light as the sun shines through that window. In the centre of the cruciform church is the altar over the tomb of St Peter, with its four pillars and the great mosaics of the evangelists; all this signifies Christ, present both in the Gospel message and in the Eucharist. The main body of the Church, the largest in the world, stands for the people of God. The larger-than-life statues beside the two rows of columns that run from end to end represent all the many founders and foundresses of religious orders, and surely must be meant to stress the charismatic function of such communities within the Church. The dome, on which the words "Tu es Petrus" are inscribed in letters of gold, broods over everything and holds everything together.

I. The Holy Spirit

Quite obviously it is not only since Vatican II that the Holy Spirit has been the 'bringer of light' to the Church. The language of holy scripture is perfectly clear, especially in Jn 14:16: "I will pray to my Father and he will send you another counsellor, to remain with you always . . . the Spirit of truth". Patristic theology always stressed this aspect and the theology of the eastern Orthodox does so to this day, so those are rightly called pneumatological theologies. But in the western Church the Holy Spirit became more and more 'the unknown God'. Here, evidently in the wake of Roman law, structure and authority were given pride of place until Pope John, moved by a sudden inspiration of the Holy Spirit, announced the Council and then repeatedly dazzled us with the prospect of a 'new Pentecost'.

Has this prophecy turned out to be an empty one? Events have not contradicted him. After the spate of secularisation — or, rather, while it still persists — an unexpected reaction has set in and men are again feeling the need for experience of God. A few years after writing *The Secular City*, Harvey Cox published *The Feast of Fools*. 'Man the master-manager' is being followed by 'post-industrial man', and this newcomer wants to celebrate feast-days and pray and endow life with a deeper meaning.

Many young people's masses — attended by adults too — last for two hours or more. And in many different places charismatic groups meet in order to pray. The 1974 Synod of bishops saw this as a typical sign of the

21

times and a clearly hopeful one; and Paul VI, in granting these movements a special audience at Pentecost 1975, put the official seal of approval on them. Some people who have studied them closely assure us that they are giving rise to a more ecumenical Church because all who pray in the Spirit know themselves to be at one over essentials and can therefore more easily overcome the differences that still exist. Furthermore we should, we are told, expect them to increase the Church's missionary consciousness because those who have experienced the Spirit feel themselves urged by the Spirit to proclaim to the whole world the mighty works of God.[2] This same Spirit has sprung a number of surprises on the Church. Indeed, given that in the work of creation he showed himself capable of limitless invention, it is only to be expected that he will be even more generous with his gifts in the realm of spiritual experience.

Religious need to be on the alert lest the laity overtake them in this movement of the Spirit and render them superfluous. The Decree *Perfectæ Caritatis* discussing renewal of the religious life puts forward (n. 2) three principles which look to the past (Christ and the Gospel, the spirit of the founder and the sound traditions of each community) and then one which looks to the future (the signs of the times). There is, however, always a danger that sheer fear will cause less stress to be laid on this last new principle and greater reliance to be placed yet again on the traditions of the past — sound and wholesome traditions, no doubt, but outdated. In point of fact the founders of the religious orders looked above all to the future, so it is by doing likewise today that we shall remain faithful to them and to their vision.

II. Christ

Every age constructs its own image of Christ. Ways of discerning and following Christ cover a wide span from the Pantokrator of the eastern basilicas to the suffering Christ carved by negro slaves in countless churches in Latin America, slaves who had recognised this man as their lifelong companion and fellow-sufferer.

Whereas traditional theology was dominated by a 'high' christology which plunged straight into teaching the Christ of dogma, the pre-existent Son of God, nowadays there is a preference for developing a 'low' christology which envisages a learning process similar to that of the apostles. In their case the all-important thing was their meeting with this strange man who, although authoritative when summoning disciples to follow him, got tired and hungry like anyone else; who championed the poor by word and deed and taught an eloquent lesson to the priests and levites whose religious traditions led them to walk straight past the man lying at the side of the road; who spent whole nights in prayer and spoke so wonderfully reassuringly about the Father in heaven; who had the courage to engage in contestation, showing the synagogue elders, the pharisees, the doctors of the Law and the high priests how gravely they misrepresented God's intentions — and who paid the price of all this when he went unresistingly to meet death, the lot of all the prophets.

Careful consideration of *this* Christ has a liberating effect, and is conducive to an effort to imitate him. Once our experience has embraced *this* Christ we become capable of the fuller experience and deeper thought that came to the apostles after Easter: we can accept the uniqueness and divinity of this man, perceiving that these do not contradict his humanity but complement it and constitute an authentic revelation. We can even become capable of confidently preaching this revelation to the world. In this way we can truly 'grow' in knowledge of our Lord and Saviour Jesus Christ (2 P 3 : 18).

III. The people of God on pilgrimage

Recognition of the laity as the nucleus of the Church, along with acceptance of 'people of God' as an authentic meaning of 'Church', was no less important an outcome of the second Vatican Council than the new readiness to have cordial relations with non-Catholic Christians and non-Christians. We have begun once more to take seriously that encyclical from the first Pope, Peter: "You are a chosen race, a royal priesthood, a people set apart to proclaim the wonderful deeds of God" (1 P 2:9).

The expression 'people of God' is a potent reminder of the nation God rescued from Egypt, freed from slavery, led for forty years through the desert and finally brought to the promised land. The God of Israel was essentially the God of the exodus. Today we too must 'set out' and 'depart', leaving behind us things cherished and familiar, and live in tents, sacrificing the *stabilitas loci* of the monk in favour of the nomadic life; we must face and accept risks during life's pilgrimage, and persevere when the original impetus slackens and fades, because for us God's promise counts more than all the adversities to be encountered day by day.

In fact the God of the exodus was at the same time the God of the covenant who remained true to his promises even when confronted by an unfaithful people, and used that sinful nation — typical of all peoples and nations — as his instrument for advancing the history of salvation. This idea can certainly be applied to life in this post-conciliar period of ours, which undoubtedly constitutes a particularly important page in the long history of salvation. Consequently we are fully justified in describing current events as an extension of the 'diary of the exodus' and interpreting them in that light,[3] just as we have every right to reaffirm today certain facts recorded in the New Testament in order to make our readers and hearers grasp that what Jesus did and said to the people of his time remains valid and true for us in our time.[4]

The Church has found once again her sense of history, and now realises that she is not called upon simply to unearth dead facts buried in her archives and proclaim them in triumphalistic accents, but to live and interpret and mould history now in the making, and regard herself as the vanguard of humanity on its pilgrimage towards God. With this perspective books of ecclesiology will cease to be learned treatises and will become aids to understanding reality lived and endowed with meaning.

III

UNIVERSAL CHURCH AND
LOCAL CHURCHES

Some of the most hotly debated questions in ecclesiology today turn on the two contrasting notions of 'universal' Church and 'local' Churches. Other problems are
naturally of more immediate concern to the Christian
as an individual — marriage, sin, death, hope in this life
and hope of eternal life. But for the Church as Church,
concern for her own equilibrium, and so for her own
internal peace in the immediate future, has to take first
place.

Until recently we Catholics spoke of the Church only
in the singular, meaning the One, Holy, Catholic and
Apostolic Church. And when we personified her as
Mother Church, we understood that expression to mean
first and foremost the Pope and the bishops through whom
the voice of the Church reached us. We had forgotten
that not only the Protestants but also the New Testament
used the word Church in the plural for the most part:
Paul wrote his letters to the Churches of Ephesus, Corinth,
Rome . . . and John addressed the Churches of Asia
Minor.

If we are to understand how matters stand at present
we must first go back a hundred years and try to appre-
ciate the first Vatican Council's position. After long discussion, that Council defined both the Pope's primacy of

jurisdiction and the conditions under which infallibility attaches to his exercise of it. However, we must not forget that the entry of Piedmontese troops into Rome on September 20, 1870, interrupted the Council's proceedings and put an end to consideration of another document, already drafted, dealing with the bishops and with the Church as a whole. Vatican I ecclesiology therefore remained incomplete and consequently one-sided. It erected only one pillar of ecclesial power, the pillar of power at the centre; and in the years that followed more and more emphasis was placed on that central power, almost as if to compensate for the Pope's loss of political power as the Church declined as a state. This led to forms of ecclesial centralism at which we can laugh indulgently today. (Think of a sick priest being obliged to seek Rome's permission, through the Nuncio, to celebrate Mass seated; or of nuns being obliged to do the same before they could wash any altar napkins not first washed by the priest). That post-Vatican I state of affairs was in some ways rather like a state of emergency which, though justifiable in periods of exceptional difficulty, ought never to become permanent.[1]

After a delay of nearly a hundred years Vatican II resumed the work which Vatican I had been unable to complete. It erected the second pillar. The Dogmatic Constitution on the Church (LG 18) says that the Council naturally confirms all the teaching of Vatican I, and that it is continuing along the same path of clarification as Vatican I in publicly declaring its teaching concerning the bishops and the local Churches.

Before any more is said the meaning of the term 'local Church' must be made perfectly clear: put simply, the 'local' or 'particular' Church is the diocese (LG 23, 27). For a long time every city had a bishop at the head of the community of believers. Later the concept was applied more broadly and on a larger scale: a patriarchate, a rite, a nation, even a continent came to be called a local Church. And now there are also narrower applications of the term: parishes, smaller groups still ("Where two or three are gathered together in my name, I am in the midst of them", Mt 18:20) and even individual families can legitimately be called Churches (LG 11).

Now for the theology. Local Churches are not simply 'particles' of the universal Church resulting from a process of atomisation; nor do they rest on the principle of subsidiarity recognising that the Pope cannot do everything himself; nor do they exist by way of a concession on the part of the Roman curia to improve its relations with the bishops . . . No. We have to speak in thoroughly positive terms and say that just as the office of Peter is continued by his successors, so the office of the apostles is continued in the bishops, who exist therefore 'by divine institution' (LG 20). The local Churches, in all the meanings we have mentioned, do not merely belong to the Church; they *are* Church. "This Church of Christ is truly present in all legitimate local communities of the faithful" (LG 26). This is one of the most important affirmations made by the Council and it needs to be emphasised and re-emphasised if it is to make its full impact on the consciousness of the faithful.

But we must straightaway insist on a second factor of equal importance — the essential factor of *koinonia*, of communion. Local Churches are the Church of Christ only when they live in communion with all the others. Otherwise they would become 'sects' in the literal meaning of the word. The ecclesial community has two dimensions, vertical and horizontal. The vertical is apparent in the relationships between the small groups and the parish, between the parishes and the diocese, between the dioceses and the Pope; the horizontal expresses itself in the concern that the Churches have for one another: they exchange visits, help each other as best they can with money and personnel, and draw pastoral inspiration from each other, thus demonstrating mutual love and strengthening their grasp of the faith they hold in common.

This theology is now a firm datum bearing the stamp

of respectability. It is based on holy scripture and on conciliar texts as well as on many dissertations by our better theologians.

Yet efforts to put it into practice meet with remarkable resistance. In some quarters old habits of thought die hard, and there are still people who think that unity is synonymous with uniformity. For them, unity is expressible only through external phenomena, not through openness to the Spirit and loving communion between all the Churches. In their eyes the universal Church takes total precedence, and all local Churches must enrol and take their allotted places in that universal Church. They see the universal Church, not the local Church, as the source and origin of unity, and would really like to turn the whole world into one colossal Church; to put it the other way round, they would like to declare the local Church of Rome to be the universal Church. In other quarters, however, one does hear it said that there are thousands of local Churches which, in the light of Vatican II and the whole of history, are entitled to possess and retain their own characteristics and not be mere reproductions of the 'Mother Church'. All such local Churches together form the one and only Church. Legitimate pluralism is fully consistent with the greatness and transcendence of Christ, impossible to confine within the bounds of one shape or form. This shows far clearer understanding of the true catholicity of the people of God (LG 13, 23).

Lumen Gentium (n. 22) states: "... the Roman Pontiff has full, supreme and universal power over the Church"; but it adds immediately: "The order of bishops ... together with its head, the Roman Pontiff, ... is the subject of supreme and full power over the universal Church". The fact that there are tensions between these two powers, these two poles in the Church is of the nature of things. One of the tasks the Council has bequeathed to us is precisely that of giving each of the two its due.

There is no denying the widespread existence at the present time of an attitude which Hans Urs von Balthasar has called 'an anti-Roman frame of mind'.[2] However, he has at the same time shown that the phenomenon is not new but has cropped up time and again all through the history of the Church; for right from the beginning there have always been tensions — between Peter and Paul, between authority and charism, between law and love, between the centre and the periphery. Such tension, he says, has to be acknowledged, explained theologically and endured; it is a salutary form of suffering. That, one can add, is not to say that the second pole, the weaker one, should forgo exercising its rights and simply sacrifice them to the centre. What has to be sought is a proper balance between Vatican I and Vatican II — not just a theological balance but a concretely effective balance of rights.

In matters liturgical we can now detect a turn of the screw. In spite of the generous norms laid down by the Council for adapting the liturgy to the genius and traditions of peoples (SC 37-40), and in spite of the encouragement given by Pope Paul VI in *Evangelii Nuntiandi* — which entrusts the local Churches with the task of transposing the substance of the Gospel message into the language their people understand (the word 'language' to be taken here not only in the semantic or literary sense but also in the anthropological and cultural sense) and of effecting this transposition in the forms and modes of liturgical expression, in catechesis, in theological formation, in secondary ecclesial structures and ministries (n. 63) — in spite of all this the 'Mass of Zaire' has just been refused approval and the 'Indian liturgy' used for some years past in India has been prohibited. One might well be tempted to say that the tragedy of the Chinese rites question is being repeated — even though on a smaller scale — and that the principle of unity in externals seems still to be the dominant one.[3] The fact that an uncompromising stand is taken against individualist extremists on both left and right is to be applauded; but the authorised middle lane, always patrolled by the bishops, needs to be seen to be broader and more varied in its surface details.

Theology, since it is less bound by rules and regulations, can be expected to give us some surprises. Until recently one continent only did all the theology; and even here only one small group of men contributed to it — the medieval theologians and their less great heirs. But nowadays Latin America, Africa and Asia all have their theological faculties and periodicals. More than that: they contain lively communities who read and live the Gospel, and thus do theology in an existential manner. From now on there is going to be theology, as well as mission, in six continents; and this will set in motion an entirely new train of events.

We have once more begun to regard the Gospel not simply as a relic to venerate or a monument to admire but as a motive force impelling us in new directions, a kind of 'nuclear energy' capable of developing still greater thrust. Just as we are in the process of exploring outer space in the physical universe, knowing full well from the start that we shall never penetrate to the farthest reaches, so too we are setting about making discoveries in what we may call the 'outer space' of theology. The formulas of the traditional manuals may retain their validity, but we are coming to realise that they certainly do not contain the full truth and that we are not obliged to keep and preserve them unchanged for ever. Beyond them we have indeed stumbled on theological outer space; and the farther we venture into it the more we realise that we shall never penetrate to the heart of it, because there dwells the God of infinite greatness who does not fully unveil his mystery while history still has its course to run through time. For exploring this outer space we need astronaut theologians, with the courage to accept the risks entailed in not saying yet again what has always been said, who will press ahead over new ground and lead us deeper into the unfathomable mystery.

This burst of theologising in all six continents can no longer be regulated and controlled from one centre pronouncing judgments of approval or prohibition case by case; any one single centre operating on those lines would inevitably be faced with an impossible task. Must we be afraid of this development and see in it a loss of substance and unity? Ought we not rather to be glad that so much importance is being attributed to it, that it conforms more closely to reality and that it is bringing such an unlooked-for enrichment of theology? Surely we can face with equanimity the prospect of 'heresies' that are simply material, not formal — errors amounting to no more than a degree of distortion in ways of approaching things and expressing things (though not, of course, of any heresy that is a conscious denial of christian truth). Such 'errors' will automatically get corrected by the time factor and by the contact theologians nowadays maintain with one another. As M. Pomiglio says in his *Il Quinto Evangelio,* every age has to write its 'own' Gospel — that is to say, preach and live the Gospel in ways that are always new.[4]

So, we ought to spend less time peering at the dangers and much more time examining the possibilities that are opening up. We ought to be grateful for this theological springtime and this outpouring of the Spirit on the Church, spurring so many local Churches to live autonomous lives and thus adorn the one single Church, the Bride of Christ, with gold and silver and garments of many colourful designs, until the fame of her beauty reaches deep into all nations (Ez 16: 13).

IV

INITIATION INTO PRAYER:
ITS PRIORITY IN CATECHESIS

If we take 'catechetical matters' to mean, primarily, questions of methodology, terminology, pedagogy, or even the content of what is taught, we do not readily identify initiation into prayer as a subject for catechetical study. But if the meaning of 'catechesis' is the meaning given to it by the bishops at the 1974 Synod, that is to say, evangelisation capable both of nourishing the faith of Christians and of arousing positive faith in non-Christians, then our list of educational top priorities must include initiation into prayer.

I would therefore like to deal with this aspect first:

I. Initiation into prayer: its place in catechesis

a) Both at the first International Congress of Missionary Catechesis, Eichstadt 1960, and at the Pan-African Congress, Katigonda 1964, the main criticism levelled at traditional catechesis was that it was too abstract, too intellectualistic, geared to faculties of mind, especially the memory, rather than to existential experience.

It would not be at all difficult to cite numerous instances of African catechists, often unable to read or write but knowing by heart the 200 or so questions and answers in the catechism, who diligently drilled their catechumens (until they too could recite everything to perfection) apparently unaware that on the lake at Genesaret Jesus taught the people in a very different fashion.

The result was that many African Christians learned about christianity but often went on practising their pre-christian religions; they ran the risk of regarding christianity as no more than a subject in the school curriculum, to be dropped as pointless once schooling and examinations were over.

Although there undoubtedly was practice of a kind, what we had — as the Italian Episcopal Conference stressed in its Synod document in 1974 — was a Church of practisers, not a Church of believers, a Church of the catechised, not a Church of the evangelised.

Those methods, then in use throughout Europe, dated back to the Counter Reformation which had given rise to a stance that was primarily defensive. The aim was a sound knowledge of the truths of the faith, so as to enable heresy to be detected and error to be refuted.

By contrast today, while orthodoxy is by no means devalued, decisive worth is accorded to orthopraxis, since "even the demons believe that, and they tremble with fear" (Jm 2: 19).

Catechesis and evangelisation ought to elicit an existential response of total self-abandonment to the Father who has revealed himself in Jesus Christ, a 'yes' to the message calling us to God's kingdom. This response in faith, hope and charity is prayer!

If the ultimate purpose of all catechesis is prayer in this sense, then catechesis has to bring about a fusion of action with contemplation; the result will be Christians who are not merely just baptised but truly believing, "holy and spotless before God, to the praise of his glorious grace which he freely bestowed on us in his beloved Son" (Ep 1: 4-6).

b) There is another consideration too. We have only just emerged from the 'Death of God' phase in theology and we still have to contend with secularisation and its concomitants — the 'silent' God, the 'absent' God, scientific man, technological man, space-age man. Yet already a fresh tide is flowing: an impulsive reaction has set in and there is a new demand for festivals, celebrations, unreasoning spontaneity, mystery, prayer.

Jesus People, Jesus Revolution, Word of God communities, Yoga, Zen, transcendental meditation, etc., are only the tip of an iceberg testifying to the existence of a vaster phenomenon — man's radical inability to be content with himself, and his innate need to transcend his own existence and take refuge in a mystery whose only adequate language is the language of prayer.

c) It became perfectly clear during the last Synod of bishops in 1974 that the Catholic Church is not out of reach of this fresh tide. Although the bishops of Latin America, Africa and Asia laid great emphasis on integral salvation and total liberation, and on social, political, temporal, 'horizontal' commitment, they all nonetheless agreed in affirming that this horizontal commitment can never be authentic, or even efficient and fully human, unless it has a vertical dimension as well — interior conversion, receptiveness to the kingdom of God, eschatological hope.

That is why the Synod spoke explicitly, in the context of evangelisation, about prayer and about the interior life.

Moreover it is highly significant that the only part of the final document to be accepted immediately was the part dealing with the Holy Spirit and explaining how, among the signs of the times, "many people are tending towards a deeper spiritual life and are being drawn to prayer; there is a renaissance of the contemplative life and a fresh appreciation of holy scripture" (n. 5). The same document further insists that "this experience of the Spirit of the risen Lord occurs not only at the beginning of the christian life but throughout that life" (n. 12).

If we also remember that during the Synod a very

well attended international charismatic group met every evening for prayer, that to mark Pentecost in Holy Year there was an international meeting of these charismatic movements in Rome, that Cardinal Suenens' book *A New Pentecost?* [1] has been enormously successful, that in a 'Directory of Catholic charismatic prayer groups' [2] 2400 such groups are listed as known (suggesting that there are more besides) — then it is obvious that this spontaneous return to prayer expresses an essential element of Church life. It is no less evident that without spiritual life there can be no authentic evangelisation and therefore no authentic catechesis affording a genuine initiation into Church life.

II. *Renewal of prayer forms*

Let us deal only with possibilities arising within the framework of catechesis, hoping all the same that any suggestions made may also have some effect on paraliturgical celebrations and even on the liturgy itself.

a) *Set prayers and prayer models*

Although we cannot approve of the traditional custom of beginning and ending every catechism session with an Our Father or some other set prayer, we certainly do not wish to condemn all types of formal prayer. Set prayers can be helpful. We all know from experience that prayer can be hard work. Praying is not child's play, a *motus primo primi,* a spontaneous natural reaction: it is an act of deliberate human choice; and it is, moreover, a christian act of which 'carnal' man is incapable: "No one can say 'Jesus is Lord' unless influenced by the Holy Spirit" (1 Cor 12:3). Now the Spirit is at work in differing degrees in different people. The more strongly one's life is influenced by the Spirit the better one prays. Thus the saints were great men and women of prayer; like Christ, and with Christ, they would pray for hours, even whole nights. Their prayers can serve as models for us too. There are all sorts of anthologies of such prayers.

The Psalms will never cease to be prayer models since they express all men's different degrees of anguish and of hope. One Psalm is all that is needed for a catechism session; it can come at the beginning, with a view to inducing receptiveness to the message of the word of God; or it can come at the end, either so as to sum up acceptance of the message in a prayer or — best of all — to express the resolve to face life in future more in the spirit of the message. The Our Father, on the other hand, is the all-embracing prayer, valid at all times, inexhaustible. St Nicholas of Flue is reputed to have said only one Our Father throughout the whole of his pilgrimage to Einsiedeln. That should suffice to make the point that set prayers of this kind should not be repeated over and over again or rattled off as a mere matter of form; they should be offered thoughtfully, treated as a celebration, savoured to the full.

Of the Our Father I would say: less often and to greater effect. In the past it was customary to recite five Pater nosters and five Aves. Nowadays we are finding that just one, said in unison by everyone present, probably makes a deeper impression than those five. The Our Father ought to be 'celebrated'. For instance, we can form a circle with the catechumens, everyone looking upwards or else with his eyes closed, hands raised — like Christ during his nights of prayer — or even pressed together; then, on behalf of the whole parish, the whole Church, the whole of humanity we can recite it slowly, or sing it. This prayer will then be a discovery, an experience, a prayer that is precious.

We can also seek out new prayer models — pre-christian ones. Man everywhere has always prayed in one way or another. Thirty years ago missionaries were in the habit of saying: "The pagan peoples of Africa have no prayers". But Fr Lufuluabo, a Franciscan of Zaire, once wrote: "At that time my mother taught me that whenever I went fishing I must always release the first fish I caught so as to thank God for taking care of us".[3] So it is up to us to explore the holy but hidden territory of non-christian prayer.

An African priest, B. Nyom, after studying biblical prayer and comparing it with African prayers, has suggested that the Church in Africa might draw inspiration from the prayers of the Bible instead of continuing to recite the abstract prayers imported by the missionaries.[4] Prayers of Latin American, African and Asian origin are to be found in a number of anthologies. Why not use them in the Church, elaborating their meaning as was done in the case of the Psalms, the full meaning of which emerged when the christian community related them to Christ?

Then too there are prayer models coming from present-day Christians who may not be saints but may well be 'inspired', writers who live today's history of salvation and express the cries of the people of God — cries of anguish for the injustices in Latin America, cries of *joie de vivre* in Africa or of gratitude for spiritual experience in Asia. We can leave it to the theologians to define the difference between inspiration in holy scripture and inspiration in modern writers (and there is indeed a difference). But no exclusivist criterion is acceptable any longer, given that the same Holy Spirit is undoubtedly at work today as well. It is up to the Church, the local Church, to judge how genuinely these texts are 'inspired', how faithfully they express christian belief, and in what ways they can therefore be used in catechesis and also in paraliturgical and liturgical celebrations.

b) *Spontaneous prayer*

So we accept that prayer models are of value. But we are even more in favour of spontaneous prayer, both individual and communal. Authentic prayer is response to God from a human person, from a personality which cannot be interchanged with that of another person and which does not express itself primarily in other people's words.

40

It is now fifty years since F. Heiler wrote, in his basic study: "Prayer among the primitive peoples is the direct expression of deep spiritual experience: it springs spontaneously from a sense of need or a feeling of gratitude; the irrepressible emotion bursts out in a free flow of words — lamentation, supplication, praise and thanksgiving..." [5]

Yet we chose to import into those countries brimming with spontaneity a bundle of stereotyped, pre-fabricated set prayers: morning prayers, evening prayers, prayer before meals, prayer after meals, act of faith, act of hope, act of charity, rosary, etc.... and in this way we stifled all their spontaneity, devaluing their precious cultural heritage instead of welcoming it into the Church and helping it to mature. In other words, we imported prayers instead of teaching prayer.

And now we find the independent churches (sects) achieving tremendous success in Latin America, Africa and Asia — a success due in large part to their spontaneous liturgical celebrations in which every person present feels both involved and at one.

It is time we realised that spontaneity is neither a disastrous bursting of the river banks nor a disgraceful lack of discipline but rather a gift from God, a sharing in his creativity and freedom, a thing to be encouraged not stifled. Then we too, being filled with the Holy Spirit, can begin to speak as the Spirit gives us utterance (Ac 2:4).

Catechesis provides the right context for teaching young Christians, and adults too, to pray in the Spirit. There are dozens of different ways of doing so, but a few hints will be enough for the moment.

Either at the beginning or at the end of the session one can ask one of those present to suggest a subject for discussion or further thought — a religious subject related either to events which have made a strong impression on the group or to what has been dealt with during the session. One can let everyone look carefully at a religious picture and think about it quietly, and then ask each one to put into a few words the thoughts it has conjured up. Instead

41

of making everyone learn by heart the passages of scripture recording the Annunciation for instance, or the parable of the prodigal son, one can get two members of the group to act the events on a little stage — and it won't be long before these people's theatrical ability comes to light.

It is also important to accustom them to praying wordlessly, that is to say remaining silent for a while, like a flower facing towards the sun (the sun being of course Christ), or like a forest echoing a call (the call having of course come from Christ), or like a man waiting for the coming of his beloved (the beloved being of course Christ). Or to praying with only a few words, just breathed at regular intervals — a basic technique in psychosomatic treatment as well as in oriental prayer; for instance: Abba, Father! Here I am, Lord! Maranatha! — words which express a wide range of frames of mind. One's feelings towards God can also be made articulate through gestures expressing joy or sorrow, perhaps rhythmically or in dancing, or using local musical instruments, and so on ...

Once people become accustomed to approaches like these, all sorts of wonderful experiences are possible; and one finds a wealth of evidence that the Holy Spirit is at work — in children as well as in adults for "your praise is chanted by the mouths of babes and infants" (Ps 8:3).

Once this new way of praying is introduced through catechesis, it will spread to families, prayer groups, para-liturgical celebrations with dialogue-type homilies, *révision de vie*, etc. ... And I hope that it will also, to some degree, spread to liturgy itself.

Obviously the official liturgy must follow a certain order. But if it is restricted to the reading, Sunday after Sunday, of what has been printed once and for all in the Roman Missal, this will — despite all post-conciliar liturgical renewal — be a fresh impoverishment, deplorable in my view. I am familiar with the third Instruction on the Liturgy, 1970,[6] which put a stop to random innovation and experimentation so as to enable the whole Church to have one universal liturgy, and also with the 1973 circular letter on the four permitted eucharistic prayers [7]; but I hope, as do a number of experts, that this measure which must have made good sense at the time will be a temporary one only and that it will not remain in force for long. I have especially in mind those countries where spontaneity is most natural, those particular Churches in three southern continents which had already composed eucharistic prayers well suited to their own religious and cultural background and which now find themselves faced with a difficult choice between loyalty to Roman authority and loyalty to their cultural heritage.

Fr Boniface Luykx, a Liturgical Commission expert before, during and after the Council, repeatedly expresses regret that the Roman Missal — with its liturgy that is classical, yes, but sober and in no way attuned to African spontaneity and African symbolic language — has been imposed on the Church of Africa.[8]

A new book by L.V. Thomas and R. Luneau [9] ends by remarking that the dearth of original African religious art, at a time when the African continent is very well represented in the art world by its writers, poets, film-makers and painters, is significant. The authors consider it of first importance to allow Africa (and the same would apply to Asia and Latin America) freedom to create her own forms of religious expression, to bring into the world the religious message which it is her mission to bear for the enrichment of the Church.

Two further remarks before I finish.

What I have managed to say about these new forms of prayer gives only a poor idea of the real thing — like an artificial flower. One needs to experience them live, in a school with a priest or sister who has the special charism of being able to teach children to pray; or in a *groupement de base*, pentecostal or not, in some city. Then one sees what is meant by the christian community at prayer; and one will probably be reassured that this way of praying is indeed ecclesial in the best sense of the word.

Now, concerning the priority prayer should have in

43

catechesis. Prayer is an end in itself, not only a means to an end. But it would be one-sided not to consider it also as a means to an end — that end being a better christian life and a more effective evangelising mission. There is, in point of fact, a very intimate bond between authentic prayer and authentic mission — intimate because it is forged by the Holy Spirit who, in both prayer and mission, prompts us to express by what we say and do what it means to be the Church.

The classic example — and the proof — of this affirmation is to be found in Acts 13: while the Church of Antioch was fasting and offering worship, the Holy Spirit said: "I want Barnabas and Saul set apart for the work to which I have called them". To those who lay themselves bare to him in prayer, God will make clear their way and their mission.

So we may certainly hope that if we give our catechumens a sound initiation into prayer, they too will grow in commitment to the task of evangelising the world of today.

V

REFLECTIONS ON EVANGELISATION
AND CULTURES

Since Vatican II there has been a profound change in the Church's missionary approach to local cultures. It is true that even in the past there was no lack of official documents advising respect for differing cultures, from Propaganda Fide's 1659 letter down to the present Pope's missionary encyclicals. But if the values enshrined in these cultures are now at last being given practical recognition instead of being shunned, this is due less to papal documents from Rome than to nationalist movements arising in the countries in question. All the same we, as Church, are now gradually becoming aware that we have a duty to help to foster these values and to absorb them, as well as to interpret theologically the ways in which national culture and national history have evolved among the various peoples.

1) *Recent studies*

For the last ten years the subject of evangelisation and local cultures has been in the forefront for discussion. All the Vatican II documents from first to last, from the Constitution on the Liturgy to the Declaration on Religious Freedom, propounded very open-minded principles about cultural pluriformity in the Church. The 1974 Synod of bishops carried this open-mindedness further, as the African bishops laid great emphasis on the right and duty of the Church in Africa to be authentically African.

Since then discussion of the subject has been pursued with vigour. The main item on the agenda for the symposium of the Episcopal Conferences of Africa and Madagascar, held in Rome in September 1975, was religious acculturation and ecclesiastical indigenisation. The basic document was a study made by Bishop James Sangu entitled *Incarnating the Church in Africa*. Following this, the subject for the International Congress of Missiology, held at the Urban University of Propaganda Fide that October, was 'Cultures and Evangelisation'; the congress proceedings now published fill three large volumes.

Conferences like these — and other meetings and study-weeks on the same subject — can give no more than a glimpse of the vital problems facing the Churches in non-western countries which have achieved political, cultural and ecclesial self-awareness and now seek new forms of self-expression. Fr W. Henkel of Propaganda Fide drew up a bibliography on this subject for the International Congress of Missiology; it listed 68 books and 183 selected articles published in the previous ten years alone.[1] There are some most promising new theological reviews edited by local scholars — for instance, one Indian one called *Jeevadhara* (meaning 'Let there be light'): *A Journal of Christian Interpretation*, Alleppey, 1971 et seq., and one in French-speaking Africa called *Telema* (meaning 'Stand up and walk'): *Revue de réflexion et créativité chrétiennes en Afrique*, Kinshasa, 1975 et seq.

At one of many study-weeks, the distinguished Professor John Mbiti gave an address to 90 experts from 36 mission countries on 'Indigenous African culture in relation to evangelisation and the Church's development'; from the subsequent discussion a consensus emerged on the following points, which I find significant in present circumstances:[2]

46

a. Cultural diversity is part of the reality of human existence. Only within the terms of his own cultural experience can a man be intelligible to himself and to others. Even the revelation and self-communication of God in Jesus Christ took a form conditioned by one particular region. But the christian religion, far from being exclusively bound up with this or that particular culture, can be lived and expressed in terms of any culture. Every culture, therefore, provides a suitable context in which to live the christian life, just as every language is a suitable vehicle for conveying the word of God to men.

b. Every culture has good and valid elements as well as sinful and erroneous ones. But it does not lie within the competence of the missionary, a foreigner, to pass judgment on the cultures of the peoples to whom he is sent, just as it is not for him but for God to pass judgment on the sinfulness or holiness of individual persons. His task is to make it easier for the Gospel, added as leaven to each culture, to bring about a gradual transformation of each culture from within.

c. It is very regrettable that a certain ethnocentrism — not an exclusively western form of blindness — has often prevented missionaries from recognising the significance and importance of cultural diversity. Yet such recognition now, if backed by constant resistance to the negative blinding influence of ethnocentrism, is bound to make the future attitudes and methods of missionaries vary widely from one distinct cultural situation to the next.

2) *Theological progress*

Now let us look at the progress theology has made in the last ten years on this question of evangelisation and cultures. As I see it there have been three rungs on the ladder of progress, and I will call them 'adaptation', 'incarnation' and 'interpretation'.

47

In the past 'adaptation' or 'accomodation' was the accepted approach. We saw the Church as the bulwark of civilisation, truth and grace. The various cultures and their real values were invited to enter the Church, and the Church for her part could meet the Gentiles half-way by allowing some adaptation of externals — behaviour, dress, language, even rites ... A recent study of the Church in Africa points out that during the second Vatican Council both missionary bishops and native bishops from Africa did in fact speak in terms of theological, liturgical and pastoral 'adaptation'.[3]

Yet at the same time the Council itself was working out a quite new way of approaching the question: 'incarnation'. The classic text is in *Ad Gentes*, n. 10:

> "The Church fully realises that she still has an enormous missionary task to perform. For two billion human beings — and their number increases daily — forming large and distinct groupings united in permanent cultural ties, ancient religious traditions and strong social relationships, have still not heard or have only barely heard the Gospel message ...
>
> In order to be able to offer to all of them the mystery of salvation and the life God has brought to men, the Church must become an integral part of all these groupings, just as Christ himself, by his incarnation, inserted himself fully into the distinct social and cultural environment of the people among whom he lived."

It is less a question of transplanting the whole of the *Corpus Christianum* than of conveying the real essence of the christian message in such a way that it will take on flesh within other cultures to form a 'new creation'. To do this, to take on shape and flesh within other cultures and so give their history a fresh start, the Church needs God's courage and Christ's *kenosis* or self-abnegation. All this is in full accord with God's creativity, leading the different cultures to *katholike*, to universality in pluriformity, enabling each local Church to find its own identity and make its own specific and unique contribution to Church dialogue through a real *koinonia* (communion).

This idea of 'incarnation' was taken up by the African bishops at the 1974 Synod in Rome, and it became the keyword in their requirements for authenticity. I will not retail all the speeches made on this subject but will simply quote from the final declaration published afterwards by the 37 bishops of Africa and Madagascar who attended the Synod. In this we read:

> "With this new outlook on mission, the bishops of Africa and Madagascar regard the theology of adaptation as having been overtaken and replaced by the theology of incarnation. The young Churches cannot any longer ignore what is a fundamental requirement. Desiring to give practical recognition to theological pluralism within unity of faith, the bishops now intend to encourage the search by every sound means for a true African theology. Such an African theology, sensitive to the fundamental aspirations of the African peoples, will lead to christianity becoming effectively incarnated within the lives of the peoples of the black continent . . ." [4]

Thus the theology of incarnation can now be considered accepted. But the transition from theory to practice, from theology to reality, has still to be made. Having christianised Africa we now have to africanise christianity in Africa. Until now we have devoted more effort to finding justification for this aim than to making concrete moves to attain it.[5]

But even in the theological field a further step forward has still to be taken. The best trends in recent thinking on our subject can be grouped under the heading 'interpretation' or hermeneutics.[6] It is no longer a question merely of enabling the values of other cultures to take root inside the Church but of giving a 'christian' interpretation to the whole reality constituted by humanity, even to those parts of that reality which are 'outside' the Church. Naturally this new thinking must not be taken to exclude the theology of incarnation but to complement it, laying stress on what is a fresh aspect of the matter. Those who are perhaps not yet prepared to accept it can at least regard it as a working hypothesis within the framework of theological pluralism.

There is nothing now to stop us from saying that christianity is not so much a system of truths as a new impulse, a new hope pinned on the kingdom of God. It is a new prophetic interpretation of human reality as that reality exists inside and outside the visible Church. The central truths lie in the fact that Christ has brought the whole of humanity into a new relationship with God: the fact that we now know, thanks to Christ's revelation, that God is loving and indeed a Father to all men (cf. the many Gospel parables); the fact that peace is now granted on earth to all men who enjoy God's favour (Lk 2:14); the fact that God wills (*"qui vult"* — not a mere wish but an effective act of will) that all men should find salvation, because there is only one God and also only one mediator between God and mankind, the man Jesus Christ who sacrificed himself to bring peace to the whole of humanity (1 Tm 2:4). Christ is indeed at work in every man and woman, and in every people, every culture and every religion. Wherever there is a man living in accordance with his convictions (that is to say, following the dictates of his conscience) and doing good to others, God is there, behind him and 'in' him: the one and only God who revealed himself in Jesus Christ. The sentence: "He came as evidence of the truth . . . to teach the nations the faith and the truth" (1 Tm 2:7) does not mean that he came to destroy the past but that he came to give the past and the present a new meaning — a christian meaning.

Since Christ, and because of Christ, we know that all men are sons of God, as Christ was at his birth. We know that we meet Christ in all men, especially the poor. We realise that all human history has become salvation history, and that the 'special case' revelation (i.e., interpretation of history) to be found in the Old and New Testaments illustrates the pattern, and at the same time constitutes the proof, of God's inspiration and abiding presence in *all* human history.

Religion, however, is not merely a matter of one hour of worship each week; nor is it something extraneous, alien to real life though wedged into it. It is the real kernel of human life; and it gives a prophetic meaning to every day of the week. The purpose of that one hour of worship is to re-awaken us to awareness of reality made new and prepare us, before God, to give generously of ourselves for others, as Christ gave himself for us.

When things are seen in this light, great progress is made towards understanding the new way of relating one's life to one's religion, and also the new way of approaching our problem of evangelisation and cultures. There is no need for the African reality to be replaced by a foreign, christian, western reality; the need is for the African reality to be interpreted and made complete by the christian revelation. In this way the African reality will be christianised from within, and all that is good and human and valid in African tradition will be preserved. We have to find a prophetic interpretation for present-day African history. For my part I look upon the effort of the last twenty years to achieve independence as a modern equivalent of the Israelite Exodus. Yahweh, the God of history, is present here too in the midst of 'his' people, for every people is his people. Efforts to achieve a better life, work in aid of human development and in defence of human dignity — these, to my mind, are authentically religious actions fulfilling the will of God and, in the final analysis, making one's life accord with faith in the Incarnation of Christ, who took the realities of human life very seriously.

Let me now leave it to you, my Lords, to your priests and seminarians and your local communities, to think over this new principle of interpretation and try to identify positive ways of moving in this direction. We must all be generous and truthful. There is one thing more important for all of us than making concrete decisions and allowing or disallowing this or that: it is achieving an inner maturity that will give our lives a new orientation, a new hope. This hope is hope in the kingdom of God, which certainly will come because it came in Christ. That, after all, is the light in which we should interpret all things.

Let us all develop a new awareness of the mystery of God. The Gospel must grow! Christ's message is far more than a string of human words; it is a leaven, a stimulus, a 'nuclear energy' whose full force has not yet been released.

Most of the African local Churches are still in their first or their early-second centuries of christianity. They are therefore experiencing what primitive christianity experienced in the days of Justin, Origen, Tertullian, etc.; for it was then that the idea of *logoi spermatikoi* was conceived, that Greek philosophy was first thought of as *paidogogos eis Christon*, and that the way was cleared for a synthesis of graeco-roman culture and the christian message.

The *kairos* has now come for the African Church to carry out a similar process. A recent book on African religions asserts that although Africans are well represented in the world of literature, painting, drama and the like, there is an unfortunate dearth of religious creativity because until now freedom in this area has been lacking.[7] The time has now come to grant this freedom, not only in theory but in practice too; for I believe that when religion cramps human freedom it does not accord with God's plan.

The time of grace has come. Christ wants to live in Africa, not as a refugee, as he lived in Egypt during his childhood, but as a full citizen, a native of the place; for wherever he comes, he comes 'to his own people' (Jn 1:11). With your trust firmly in him, you will assuredly build up the African Church of the future.

VI

EVANGELISATION IN PRESENT-DAY CONFLICT-PRONE SOCIETY

This last quarter of the twentieth century is according us the singular privilege of witnessing a new phenomenon — conflict-prone society.

Throughout history there have always been conflicts of one kind or another. But the current state of affairs — with the world abounding in crime, exploding with it in fact, and with present-day society so characterised by conflict that to speak of it as conflict-prone is no exaggeration — does constitute a new phenomenon, a product of modern man.

The Italians have a word for it: *conflittualità*. Originally coined in syndicalist circles to express the 'inevitability of conflict' by which strike action was justified, it is now used more broadly since strikes are no longer the most obvious manifestation of conflict-proneness.

Within present-day society there is a great deal of strife far more heated and far more discordant than strike action. There are rapes and muggings, murders and suicides, hijackings and kidnappings, sexual crimes, political crimes using bombs, dynamite and Molotov cocktails, etc. . . . . One has only to read the newspapers: every day there are more lines in bold type reporting acts of violence, no longer committed just sporadically by individuals but organised *en masse* and carried out with systematic regularity. The more talk there is of laws and measures to combat crime and delinquency, the more these spread and extend their reign of terror. Until now, each time we have hoped that the violence had reached its peak and would decrease our hopes have been disappointed.

The phenomenon is not confined to Italy, a country characterised until recently by its very strong family and Church traditions, the virtual collapse of which has brought the country to the opposite extreme. Other countries run the Italian record very close or even beat it. A recent report asserts that four murders and 971 other crimes occur daily in New York City alone, and that crime rose 9.2% in 1974 compared with the previous year.

And what can one say of the young countries of the Third World, where the gaiety and dancing of the independence celebrations have been abruptly superseded by disillusionment, tribalism, *coups d'etat,* civil war? First it was the Congo and Biafra, then Bangla Desh, Vietnam, Mozambique and Angola. Today we are anxiously watching what goes on in Lebanon and Rhodesia. And tomorrow?

But what of ourselves, we churchmen? We too are in this state of being conflict-prone. And it is this condition of ours that is the most grievous wound in the Body of Christ, so deeply deplored by Pope Paul in his Apostolic Exhortation of December 8, 1974, *Paterna cum benevolentia,* appealing for unity within the Church.

Many priests are living in a state of continual tension, not merely because of the celibacy issue but because of a feeling of lost identity, because of inability to reconcile science with ecclesiastical authority, because of dissension within the priesthood itself and everywhere among the people of God. We have the 'left' and the 'right', the 'young' and the 'old', the 'progressives' and the 'conservatives'.

And it is a real tragedy that groups of people committed to living the Gospel in a truly radical fashion quite often lose hope in the Church and come to believe that they must join one or other of the sects.

In all this one does indeed glimpse, sense, become aware of something of the mystery of iniquity!

Perhaps what I have said is pessimistic; certainly it is one-sided, because both in the Church and in society there is so much that is positive. But now we are going to shine a little light right into the darkness of this conflict-prone existence of ours.

There is a paradox, and it is this: the condition of conflict-proneness is favourable ground, theologically, for evangelisation. By this I mean not only that it creates just the environment into which the good news most needs to be inserted, but that it is the premiss which allows the true meaning of evangelisation to be understood; or — in other words still — it is a constitutive element with which evangelisation becomes fused, as matter is with form.

The Church exists for the sake of the world, not vice-versa. It is her duty to ponder where and how and why this world is in darkness, crumbling into ruins and lacking salvation. But it is the world, not the Church, that decides the order of the day; so it is in clear response to the needs of the world that the Church has to understand herself as the sacrament of salvation.

This world in ferment, conflict-prone, is therefore — I would say — 'ideal' ground in which to sow the seed of the Gospel and nurture it.

It is true that the Church is never free from the temptation to indulge in nostalgia for the lost earthly paradise: there is a tendency to idealise, to 'hagiographise' reality, whereas reality is in fact harsh and ugly. All the same, the Church has to enter into this reality and accept it for what it is, not with passive resignation but with willingness to make allowances; she must take up reality's challenge and win the day through evangelisation.

Evangelisation is certainly not a magical treatment capable of working miracles, but it can and should make a contribution to overcoming conflict-proneness by therapy.

The first step in the therapeutic process must be to arrive at an accurate explanation of the phenomenon. Diagnosis is essential to healing, or at least to better understanding of the condition. Viewed in relation to evangelisation, the present-day proneness to conflict becomes more than just a product of the political, economic and ecclesiastical situations now prevailing. Behind the visible facade there lurks the agent-in-chief — a sinister and terrible power to which man, incapable of putting up a strong resistance, too often and too easily falls victim. Whether we call it sin or the devil or the mystery of evil, etc., matters very little. The fact remains that this power does exist; it is stronger than man, and mankind does have to struggle not only against human forces but against the principalities and powers who are the masters of this world's darkness, against the spirits of evil everywhere in the universe (Ep 6: 12).

Nowadays sin is no longer thought of mainly as something occurring in individuals, something capable of being pinpointed and analysed within the personal conscience; it is also thought of as something objectivised, something incarnated in structures and in political and social injustice, in the conflict-prone situation of which man is at one and the same time both the author and the victim.

So, 'the sin of the world', 'original sin', can surely now be regarded not so much as an incident that took place 500,000 years ago but more as a reality in our everyday lives.

Yet the situation is not hopeless because "God anointed Jesus of Nazareth with the Holy Spirit and with power; and wherever he went he did good, healing all those who had fallen into the power of the devil" (Ac 10: 38); and our firm conviction that we have been ransomed and set free from that evil power may be the prime contribution that evangelisation can make to the therapy. Now that he is no longer obliged to lean on fixed tradition's crutches, man is more free to move; no doubt he can become worse, but he can also become better, and indeed come to be true to his inner nature — the nature of a being created in the image and likeness of God!

Evangelisation draws back the curtains, not only those concealing the recesses inhabited by the 'dark' power in man but also those preventing the light that is nonetheless in him from shining brightly outwards.

Man is God's creation, and he has been redeemed by God! No man or woman is totally ugly or totally bad. And among men there are no brute beasts, even if the press does talk far too much about those human beings it chooses to describe as brutes.

It is up to us to discover, behind the acts of brutality, the desires, aspirations and legitimate worries of the people in question. In the end, behind all the sins and aberrations of modern man — subhuman and superhuman, anarchic, sex-obsessed, demon-possessed — we shall find a profound human need that is still unmet. Conflict-proneness, being a real-life phenomenon, will never be overcome until the need at the back of the aberration finds its true satisfaction.

The Church must always remember that it is no part of her duty to compile a dossier on the evils of the age or pronounce sentence or join the chorus of prophets of doom, but that it does fall to her to point out and stress the fundamental goodness and kindness in man and to take man's aspirations seriously. Although one cannot approve of any acts of political terrorism, one can be impressed by the daring, the commitment and the conviction of the men behind them. There is such a fund of good intentions to be turned to good account.

Let us go a step further in our search for a therapy. Once we have this new basic approach, dialogue will be easier — and dialogue is the only way that can lead eventually to conflict-proneness being cured. Violence generates counter-violence and only produces escalating violence. We need to achieve an inner maturity that will prompt us to engage determinedly in dialogue to which we bring both full commitment and total frankness. If this is lacking there will never be any true reconciliation.

Dialogue does not mean convincing one's interlocutor of the rightness of one's own convictions; it means admitting the relativity both of one's own position and that of the other. Polarisation is definitely out of place, for the need is to bridge the psycho-sociological gap between the different understandings, which as a rule are not alternative but complementary understandings of the problem. To arrive at the truth each needs the other.

Clearly this presupposes an inner flexibility. There has been much wrangling in the Church, and not so long ago either, precisely because flexibility was lacking; yet flexibility ought to be a characteristic of all who listen to the Holy Spirit who 'blows where he pleases' (Jn 3:8). To take one example: twenty years ago Fr Rahner was forbidden to write any more about the idea of concelebration, and Frs Congar, de Lubac and Chenu were all dismissed from their posts as teachers of theology. Yet those 'dissenters' prepared the way for Vatican II and had a strong influence on its work, all of which has set the Church on a completely fresh course greatly to our liking.

Such recollections teach us that while there is a need for dissent on the one hand there is a need for patience on the other — a need for elasticity in order to avoid fractures and for the courage to allow time to bring about a gradual evolutionary process. A degree of compromise is not always a sign of cowardice; on the contrary . . . It is common courtesy, mutual deference for the sake of keeping the peace and preserving the unity and the highest values of the Church. It is not a sign of weak submission but of hope, because we believe that good will eventually triumph over evil and that history does not run a course that is meaningless.

There is one more consideration in this context: inner personal conversion and changes in structures are interdependent. Both are necessary in the effort to build a better world and a better Church. "YOU ought to change for the better", otherwise changed structures will merely mean that a new stage has been erected but that the actors and the parts they play have remained exactly as before.

But structures too must really change; otherwise man will grow weary and feel frustrated in spite of all his goodwill.

So both need to change!

However, the signs of the times suggest that whereas one turn of events will be more conducive to inner conversion, patient endurance and hope, another will call for harder work to bring about a real change of structures.

The therapy we envisage will prove laborious, but the Church has one incomparable asset, one inexhaustible reserve of strength to draw on — her firm trust in the power of the victory of Christ. It is true that many people in the Church show little sign of possessing it; many in fact show signs of a curious powerlessness, a spiritual paralysis. They realise that something is wrong but don't know what to do about it. They live in fear and trembling because of the fall-off in vocations, the changes within the Church, the advance of communism. They have lost sight of the principles of action. Not surprisingly, for an atmosphere of world-weariness produces no fresh ideas; immobility and lack of fresh air only make matters worse.

We could do with a fresh intervention by the Spirit of Jesus to give the Church courage, vigour and that confident trust which gives rise to sound intuitions and initiatives leading to great undertakings.

The Church can counter the gloomy ballad of the world's woes with a cheerful song of her own. The Church, like Christ and thanks to Christ, is God's 'yes' to man (cf. 2 Cor 1:18) — to all men and to the whole of human history — which generates hope no matter how hopeless the situation may be.

The Church is the universal sacrament of salvation (her own favourite definition often repeated by the Council) for all men, Christians and non-Christians, white and black, illiterates as well as astronauts. What an assignment! So much trust to be instilled, so much reassurance to be given. . . .

But let us not forget that the Church does not consist only of the Pope and the bishops. We too, with them, are the Church, called to radiate light in the darkness, to conquer all defeatism, to find a way out of the vicious circles set up by every manifestation of proneness to conflict.

Pope Paul VI set a shining example of hoping against hope in his Bull of Indiction of the Holy Year. At a time when everyone was clamouring for more severe measures to combat crime he dared to speak of clemency, and not only appealed to criminals to turn over a new leaf but also appealed to the civil authorities to take a first step towards reconciliation by declaring some form of amnesty. He wrote: "We should also like to express the humble and sincere wish that in this present Holy Year too, in accordance with the tradition of previous Jubilees, the proper authorities of the different nations should consider the possibility of wisely granting an amnesty to prisoners, as a witness to clemency and equity, especially to those who have given sufficient proof of moral and civic rehabilitation, or who may have been caught up in political and social upheavals too immense for them to be held fully responsible". Here we have a concrete example of evangelisation in a conflict-prone society. It is an echo of the language of Christ who came to save not the virtuous but sinners (Mt 9: 13).

Before I come to my last point, let me make one observation: salvation is for all men, and the desire to escape from this wretchedness, this condition of being conflict-prone, is universal.

So our evangelising efforts cannot be directed to our own country alone. We live in solidarity, both human and ecclesial, with the whole of humanity; so every introverted attitude, every narrowing of horizons to take in only our own problems, not only sins against the concept of salvation but also hinders us in solving our own problems

— precisely because our horizons lack breadth and we ourselves lack the right motivation.

Practical awareness of the Third World and the Third Church should not be thought of primarily in terms of granting aid and carrying an extra burden; it should be regarded as a real sharing that enriches the efforts of humanity as a whole and the Church as a whole. In such a perspective our problems acquire a new dimension and a new relativity; and although the western Church is today passing through a kind of crisis after a long period of glorious achievement, the birth and growth of the Third Church can give us an injection of courage and generate a new apostolic spirit in the Church.

Until now we have been discussing proneness to conflict and evangelisation as a means of overcoming it. The specific remedy is reconciliation. Conflict-proneness and reconciliation are correlative terms and also mutually exclusive terms. Reconciliation is the dawn that lights up the dark night of conflict-proneness and heralds the new day.

Besides making the efforts we undoubtedly must make, let us always remember that Christ won through, that he is our reconciliation, our peace, and that God wants all things to be reconciled through him (Col 1:20; Ep 2:14). 2,000 years ago the Redeemer was born at a time when, under Caesar Augustus, "all the world was at peace"; today he has to come to a world in disarray, conflict-prone — a world that has all the greater need of him.

The certainty of our faith in eschatological salvation, and in definitive reconciliation in Christ in his kingdom, gives us the courage we need to take fresh initiatives to further man's temporal salvation now and in the future. We can no longer content ourselves, as we did in the past, with praising the patience and the hope we found among the poor; for that would be 'alienation' in communist jargon and betrayal or denial in christian parlance, because every Christian who is neglectful and egoistic towards the poor, the sick and the sinful is denying the Christ in them. Christ himself brought not only hope of heaven to the poor, the sick and the sinful, but also the help they longed for in the here and now — as a pledge, an earnest and a foretaste of his kingdom's treasure. From now on we would do well to direct our christology less towards studying the abstract Christ of the first Councils and more towards examining Christ's day to day contacts with others, his challenges to the pharisees and the priests, his sympathy with the poor, his *kenosis* and self-abnegation, his total self-abandonment to the Father.

We shall then have a model not so much to venerate as to imitate, and by our imitation of him we can become rays of hope for a christian triumph over 'conflictuality'.

VII

MISSION: ITS PAST AND PRESENT

Handling this subject is rather like conducting a party of pilgrims around the Vatican museums within the space of an hour. It can be done, but a whole day or even a week could be profitably devoted to making the same tour.

If one considers the vast range of mission history, the 'gesta Dei per Francos' and other nations, the 'gesta Dei per Jesuitas' and other orders and missionary institutes, and if one also remembers the many bright spots on the missionary horizon now, it will be obvious what I mean. The only way to deal with a subject like this in the time at my disposal is to give some pointers and resort to short cuts and deliberate omissions.

So I do not propose to run through the whole of mission history, or give a panoramic survey of mission at the present time, or enumerate a host of facts or offer you a mixed bag of bright ideas. I prefer to study the implications of one single idea; and I therefore propose to point out the various factors in missionary activity and then show that mission has always been subject to change, that the changes which have taken place recently augur well, and that we can therefore face the future with confidence. In other words: historical facts — pastoral interpretation — existential approach.

I. The bearers of the message

These are the agents, the representatives, the envoys, the missionaries — and mission would be non-existent were it not for their initial thrust. In the early centuries they were first the apostles, the privileged witnesses who had themselves seen the Lord, then bishops and monks, merchants and soldiers, and above all the whole christian community in its entirety. Every young Church at once became a bridgehead for conveying christianity to the hinterland. The call to follow Christ was understood not as a privilege but as a command to impose on oneself unconditionally, just as Christ placed himself at the service of the kingdom of God.

All this generated a thrust without parallel. Even Adolf von Harnack[1] never ceased to marvel at it. Augustine wrote: "One cannot but suppose that miracles brought about the foundation and spread of christianity; its spread is perhaps the greatest miracle of all".

Once the Age of Discovery came, mission went overseas. Responsibility for it was perforce delegated, first to the Spanish and Portuguese crowns and later to the missionary institutes. Undoubtedly this resulted in an effective division of labour but at the same time it provided the Church with an alibi. One still has clear memories of missionary institutes being obliged in some instances to collect money and look for vocations without any support from bishops and parish priests — often in fact against their express wishes.

Vatican II has brought mission back '*in medio Ecclesiæ*', declaring it to be the truly vital function of the Church and indeed her *raison d'être*. The first chapter of the Decree *Ad Gentes* describes the essentially dynamic aspect of the Blessed Trinity and the way in which all members of the Church are drawn into that structure of love. Priests, and the catechists they paid, had to some extent monopolised mission for too long. Now we are getting back to the original understanding — to 'spontaneous expansion' on the part of the Church whole and entire. During the 1974 Synod of bishops, called to discuss 'Evangelisation in the modern world', something significant happened. To begin with, all the talk was of different groups of people to be evangelised — workers, students, women, etc. Then discussion took a fresh turn — a welcome one — after which all the stress was laid on the fact that the groups to be evangelised ought themselves to be the evangelisers. The Synod realised that the best way to appropriate the Gospel oneself is to convey it to others.

At this point I would be glad if I could help to overcome a temptation we continually have to face — the parish that wants thoroughly to renew itself first of all and not to engage in any missionary activity until later. There are three reasons why this is a great self-delusion: first, because we can never succeed in renewing ourselves completely; second, because renewal applied to a Church that lacks mission would be renewal applied to a pseudo-Church, and thus no renewal but a lapse into heresy; third, the best way of renewing oneself is through mission!

So mission has ceased to be something that can be hived off. Every local Church ought to be a missionary local Church. Until now only one continent, strictly speaking, has carried out a full missionary programme in four others. What an explosion of missionary activity we can look forward to, now that every local Church in every continent is going to become a missionary Church! Reports from episcopal conferences in Latin America, Africa and Asia in the last few years provide grounds for hope. Whereas before they used to talk principally about schools, money and relations with the government, now they are talking mainly about openness, dialogue and witness. So the recent transformation is very much for the better. Not that the change is yet complete, far from it! But at least a new outlook has been acquired, and the challenge it represents has been perceived.

II. The hearers of the message

At one time they were known as 'objects' of mission. But in fact they are not simply those to whom something happens; they are 'subjects', partners, called to declare their own personal reaction to Christ. 'All the nations' are to be told. A fantastic task entrusted to the apostles. A task they may well have thought ought not, strictly speaking, to be imposed on them at all. A task which, if it was to be properly undertaken and understood, called not only for intelligence but for charism as well.

And yet in actual fact evangelisation did reach out to one nation after another, and one group of people after another devoted themselves to it. To begin with it made headway within the area of græco-roman culture. The bearer of the message had no 'civilising' mission to perform there, nor could he offer any accruing worldly advantage. He offered 'nothing but' religion — as a radical decision, a genuine 'conversion' of life, a complete change of direction so as to reach the kingdom of God.

The prototype of mission then was Paul. We can imagine him arriving one day in Ephesus — the fourth largest city in the Roman empire, famous for its trade and its cult of Diana — and walking up the Via Sacra leading to the great amphitheatre; he was no tourist but a 'partisan' with a well-thought-out plan in his head. He made discreet contacts here and there, founded what nowadays would be called a *groupement de base* — a group which gradually expanded so that three years later, when the devotees of Diana provoked a rising against him and drove him out, he was able to leave behind him a well-knit community with a bishop at its head. At that time the Gospel was welcomed chiefly by the poor, the insignificant and the slaves, who found in it a message of hope; and it was through them that it often reached the lady of the house and the master.

Next on the scene were the Germanic peoples, the 'barbarians' whom Augustine anxiously expected to bring with them the end of Rome and the end of the world; but they proved good allies who, by fusing Roman culture and the christian spirit, prepared the ground for the late-mediæval flowering. There is a lesson here, valid for every age, on how to find prophetic interpretations of the somersaults history can perform.

The Age of Discovery ushered in other 'barbarians', 'savages', 'primitives' and 'pagans', — insults that nowadays we scarcely dare to breathe but that were calmly used for centuries. Our European and christian sense of superiority so blinded us that we regarded as savages all who lived beyond our cultural pale, and we ended up by exaggerating out of all proportion the cultural differences existing between them and us. Throughout that period the missionary carried with him both religion and civilisation, above all through schooling. I have not the slightest intention of denying the good intentions of those missionaries or of decrying their cultural and charitable achievements. But if one looks back on it all with a critical eye, one has to admit that religion was then an 'extra' thrown in, that becoming a Christian meant climbing up the social ladder, and that mission therefore met with most success among the poor, the sick and the no-caste. The cultured peoples of Asia, for their part, said 'thank you' to our offer and let it be clearly understood that they could do very well without it.

In the meantime the 'primitives' have become fully fledged men, and in many countries the mission schools and hospitals have been taken over by the state, nationalised. So the means and the tools of mission are being taken out of our hands. Some see this as a crushing blow to mission, but others consider it a stroke of good fortune because now we are obliged to adopt a new and less condescending missionary stance, building up christianity through mature communities with a life of their own instead of turning our attention mainly to the sick and to children and introducing christianity as if by stealth. After all, we cannot reduce God to baby-sitter rank. He wants his word to be heard by mature adults in their prime.

So here again we have an opportunity to do better things, though not easier things. We are called upon to offer a more genuine and more credible christianity.

III. Mission's environment

Environment can be either favourable or hostile to mission. Jesus found a world of difference between Galilee, with its hills and lake and kindly people, and Jerusalem, the city of authoritarianism and hardness of heart.

In the early centuries mission progressed within the Roman empire, under the mantle of the *Pax Romana,* along the roads cut for the Roman soldiery. In spite of the persecution inflicted on Christians conditions were in many respects favourable to the rapid spread of the Gospel.

From the Age of Discovery onwards mission could move and develop only under the umbrella of the colonial system then prevailing throughout the world; first there were Spanish and Portuguese colonies, then English, French, German and Belgian ones. Not wishing to make any rash assertions or point accusing fingers at any particular spot, let us simply say that mission lived in co-existence with colonialism. The system was felt on the whole to be favourable to mission since it provided a certain security, and more than a few missionaries would have welcomed its survival. We now know that we must no longer try to idealise colonialism. The contacts and exchanges between Europe and the other continents most certainly did a great deal of good, but they ought not to have developed in the way they did.

Meanwhile we have lived through the historic — and quite unique — process of de-colonisation. Thirty years ago Britannia still ruled the waves, from Gibraltar to Port Said, from Aden to Singapore. Thirty years ago 45% of humanity still lived under a colonial regime; today all those peoples have become independent states.

So now, for the first time, mission has to operate in

independent states, with all the risks that entails, with missionaries already expelled from here and there and with the threat of expulsion ever present. In no country can we offer any guarantees for the future. This causes missionaries grave psychological unease; for although journeys to and from overseas now take only hours instead of weeks, missionaries feel further away than before, in lands that are truly foreign to them.

All the same, the new situation has its possibilities. Only now can we vitalise genuinely local Churches, fully valid and alive to what they are. It is indeed a pleasant surprise to find the local bishops increasing not only in number in recent years but in quality too. It would be extremely interesting to compare the rather reserved attitude of the African and Asian bishops during the second Vatican Council with the part they played during the Synod of bishops in 1974. The Synod was as good as an open sesame for the Third Church. Although we must not minimise the difficulties facing those young Churches, we do know that because of those difficulties, because of persecution even, they are on their way to attaining maturity in Christ; we know too that difficulties are a 'must' in salvation history and that Emmaus never ceases to be an up-to-date reality. So once again we can conclude that the changes have been for the better.

IV. Mission's purpose

I do not intend to plunge into the academic discussion still going on between the schools of thought represented by Munster, Louvain and Rome (a discussion which even Vatican II did not fully resolve, for what emerged then was a compromise) as to whether the true and proper purpose of mission is preaching the faith or founding Churches. In any case we nowadays shy away from any form of ecclesiocentrism. The Church is not an end unto herself. She does not exist for her own greater glory but for the sake of the world. She is the sign of God's love for the world. Consequently her task is to proclaim the message of the kingdom of God, to evangelise, to 'shalomise'. Salvation is nowadays no longer thought of as supernatural salvation only, in terms only of faith, the sacraments and hope of eternal life; salvation is now seen to encompass man's whole existence as he lives, as he suffers and as he hopes in the here and now; and it is seen to entail total liberation from political oppression and inhuman exploitation. Nowadays we perceive the great sin to lie in the egoism, whether of individuals or of groups, that lurks in situations still awaiting salvation. Even religious ought to ask themselves whether they are not over-concerned about their distractions during prayer and their infractions of the rule of silence, and under-concerned about their lack of interest in and lack of compassion for the sufferings of humanity.

Evangelisation and humanisation are not at odds with one another, nor do they compete with one another. I would go so far as to say that, properly understood, they are synonymous. Genuine evangelisation does indeed give mankind *joie de vivre,* courage to face life and concrete help in living it. Genuine humanisation, for its part, amounts in effect to evangelisation because it conveys the Gospel not by word but by deed. Moreover it can pave the way for explicit confession of the faith, because it would not take man fully seriously as a human being if it did not also take into account his transcendental aspirations.

So yet again let us repeat that the new convictions have brought a change for the better. They restore relevance to religion: from being something on the fringes of life taking up one hour a week in church, religion becomes the soul, the meaning and the impelling force behind all the legitimate aspirations of modern man. The purpose of that hour of liturgy on Sundays is to bring us together to listen to the word, meet the Lord, become aware of how the Lord wills the salvation of all men and prepare ourselves once again to collaborate with him in a meaning-

ful way throughout the week so as to further the salvation
he wills.

V. *Pastoral balance sheet*

Christianity has penetrated country after country, continent after continent, in ever fresh waves. K.S. Latourette [2]
has shown how the Church has always overcome her own
difficulties and internal crises by pursuing new missionary
initiatives. Here is the clue to how we can overcome the
present crisis!

On the credit side we have the fact that five of the
six continents have become christian: Europe, the two
Americas, Australia and now Africa too, which in the
year 2000 will be 46% christian, or if we consider black
Africa only, 57%. Only Asia now remains. By no means a
small remainder, because that continent is the home of
54% of the world's population and, if one excludes the
Philippines, it is only 0.95% Catholic (although to include
the Philippines would bring the figure to 1.5% christian).
Will the Church register more success in Asia in future by
using new methods, or will Asia continue to remain outside
the Church, content to be a partner, albeit a counter-
attraction, in order to make manifest the absolute freedom
with which God calls and the freedom of man to respond?

Christians of all kind make up 30% of the world
population. There is still a gigantic task ahead of us.
Evangelisation is our duty; and it is within our reach now
that so many possibilities lie open thanks to the commu-
nications media, dialogue and Bible distribution — even
if we can never be sure that this evangelisation will lead
to full christianisation and the enrolment of believers into
the christian community through the sacraments. That we
must leave trustfully to God.

In saying that five continents have become christian
I am certainly not running away from the disquieting
questions raised by the degree to which those continents

show ugly signs of rapidly becoming 'post-christian'. We are back again where we started. Once again the Lord issues his command: "Go...". And today too, if we are to understand what he wants of us, we need not only intelligence but charism as well.

To sum up, we can say that from now on the Church's existence everywhere will depend on personal decisions, that christianity will be a freely chosen faith instead of being a social convention and that Christians will constitute the diaspora not the 'christian masses'. Consequently the Church will meet with opposition both from without and from within, as the Lord predicted. Nonetheless it is a Church that rejoices, not one that fears for its life and reacts by curling up inside a ghetto or a bunker, hedgehog-like. It is a Church of joy and trust, sure of the presence of the Lord and of his future *parousia*.

Two further thoughts in conclusion:

a) The 2000 years of mission history have shown us that forms can change but that mission itself goes on. That has become clearer than ever in the course of the transformation taking place in the last twenty-five years. These have left intact all that is essential and have thrown even more light on one fact: the Church, as universal sacrament of salvation, has a mission to the world. The Church will survive for the next twenty-five years and more besides, because so long as there are men on earth they will always be hungry for salvation, always wondering about life's meaning, always conscious of an interior void, always a prey to frustration and always grateful to anyone who brings them a message of hope.

b) While affirming our confident hope let us not shut our eyes to reality, to the crisis, to the scepticism now prevailing in regard to Church and to mission. We must not indulge in any illusions. One thing only is necessary: we have to steady ourselves by leaning on the word of God and experiencing the support that gives us in time of need.

Let us take Mark 16: 9-20:

Verse 11: Mary Magdalen has seen the risen Lord and reported this to the apostles, but they do not believe her.

Verse 13: the disciples from Emmaus reappear and tell of their experience, but they too are not believed.

Verse 14: finally the Lord appears to them all when they are gathered together and reproaches them for their unbelief and hardness of heart. Then immediately, without any preliminaries or discussion of any kind:

Verse 15: he says to them: "Go out to the whole world . . ."

Verse 20: and they went out and preached everywhere. The Lord was working with them and he confirmed what they said by the miracles that followed.

So: the risen Lord gives his disciples work to do and conquers their incredulity through mission. The best way to evangelise ourselves is to evangelise others!

All the same, let us constantly bear in mind that it is not we who will overcome the crisis and the unbelief but the risen Lord; and he will do it precisely through the missionary task he entrusts to us. And today too there could be 'miracles' should miracles be needed. Indeed, those who keep their eyes open can already see signs of an amazing renewal in the Church. Even today "the arm of the Lord is not too short to save" (Is 59: 1).

VIII

MISSION: ITS FUTURE

What lies ahead in mission is no less fascinating a subject than what lies ahead in exploration of outer space. In both these fields we have barely started out, and the further we go the more clearly we perceive that the task is unending.

There are various angles from which to approach our subject but I will touch on just a few:

A. From *the viewpoint of theology* we could formulate a thesis thus: mission has a future, a future guaranteed by God; mission has an historical future and it has an absolute future. On the latter we can naturally only pin our hopes, whereas the immediate future of mission is within tangible reach.

B. From *the viewpoint of religious sociology* we could make two important assertions:

The Third Church has arrived. This is *the* major event of Church history for the near future. To sum up in a few words: the first millennium of christianity was the age of the First Church, the Church of the east; in the second millennium the stage was held by the Second Church, the Church of the west; the forms christianity takes in the coming third millennium will in the main be determined by the Third Church, the Church of the southern hemisphere — Latin America, Africa, Asia.

From now on we shall no longer be able to say: here we have the Church, there we have missions. We shall of course be able to distinguish differing situations within the Church, some requiring above all a pastoral approach, others an ecumenical one, others a missionary one. But these differing situations will no longer mark out one country from another or one continent from another. So the motto "Mission in six continents" will become more and more apt.

C. From *the viewpoint of pastorality* we could complete what was said in the previous paper (VII) by adding two postulates:

The christian communities now growing up will have far fewer church buildings in the traditional style. We ought therefore to be turning our thoughts towards buildings designed to serve several purposes, not just as an economy measure but for sound theological reasons. For the christian community is not and must never become merely a cult community; it has to be much more than that, so it ought to talk over its real-life problems in its own community room and use that same room for its Sunday celebration of the Eucharist — which is its heart and its summit.

Similarly there are going to be far fewer priests of the traditional type at our disposal, especially as those we have are concentrating on the cities and major centres, leaving people in outlying areas to their fate. Here — and again not just as an economy measure but for sound theological reasons — we ought to envisage the possibility of 'proven men', good catechists, being able to preside over the celebration of the Eucharist in those outlying areas; this would tend to give the traditional image of the priest a less monopolistic look. The 1971 Synod did not say the last word in this connection.

D. Let me now put to you another angle of approach which I would like to explain more fully: *the strength of the new ideas and their effect on mission in the future.* Yes, those 'outrageous' new ideas. However, by no means all of them merit that epithet. And their newness is only relative: most of them can be found in patristic theology. But with the passage of time they got buried under a thick layer of dust and have only recently come to light again.

In any case, the maxim that ideas rule the world is always valid. Many of these new ideas have already taken root, even if their effects are not yet fully felt. They are like multi-stage rockets, in that their full capability becomes evident only little by little. So let us examine these ideas and the influence they are having, and project forward the lines along which they are already tending to develop. Instead of clinging to the *status quo* and to conditions as they now are, we would do well to take into account conditions as they may develop, as they ought to develop and as they probably will develop. If we do, we shall acquire the flexibility we are going to need, and the future will not take us by surprise and lay us low.

There is one clear lesson to be learned from our experience up until now — that we never think radically enough about the transformations taking place in the Church and in the world, that we never think imaginatively enough; as Prof. D. Wiederkehr is always saying: "Ecclesiological thinking in the Church will never catch up with the Spirit's inventiveness and knows that the Spirit will always outstrip the thinkers".[1] Of course the Spirit's creative inventiveness will always operate in complete freedom, so we would be well advised not to make rash predictions about the future of the Church. Just as the Spirit can always create something new within the Church, so he can always cause any new development to change course *en route*. But if any tendencies directly contrary to these new ideas were to assert themselves, we would have to suppose that those tendencies did not originate with the Spirit; for the Holy Spirit cannot contradict himself. And the ideas we are now discussing clearly did originate with him because they are all rooted and grounded in the second Vatican Council. Consequently their flowers and their fruits can equally be regarded as coming from him.

I. The idea of local Churches

Hitherto Catholic terminology has known of only one Church, in the singular — the One, Holy, Catholic, Apostolic and Roman Church. Protestants on the other hand used the word mainly in the plural, and so were closer to biblical usage.

The bishops of the Third Church, while not wishing to damage in any way their communion with the rest of the Church, want more decentralisation, more autonomy, more genuine realism not only in documents and fine speeches but also in practice. If we were to stiffen our resistance to this, we would run the risk of a break, as often before in history. If on the other hand we show foresight and yield ground with sympathetic understanding, there is every chance of saving what is essential. Uniformity is less of a guarantee than a danger to the genuine unity of the Churches. The future clearly will move in the direction of unity in pluriformity. We must be ready for some surprises in the near future.

II. The idea of freedom of conscience

The Decree dealing with this, *Dignitatis Humanae*, was the last to come out of the Council; it had to overcome serious obstacles while it was being finalised, and even today it meets with fierce resistance when put into practice. Yet, as Karl Rahner has said, the idea of freedom of conscience will have a far more profound effect on the future of the Church than the idea of episcopal collegiality, which is generally considered the greatest victory the Council won.

The idea of freedom of conscience does not mean that one is free of all obligation; it expresses something far nobler — that every man, being made in the image and likeness of God, has a dignity of his own and a creative freedom of his own. Each one of us is an original, not a dreary copy. Each one of us has the right to be spontaneous, to be free to make decisions according to our conscience without having other people making our decisions for us or imposing their decisions on us.

Freedom of conscience obviously presupposes a degree of maturity. It has to develop. So we have to make sure that we give man the opportunity to develop it. Missionaries have far more important things to do than to dictate sets of rules prescribing which of the traditional customs are prohibited and which permitted: what mission has to do is to help Christians to attain inner maturity and so learn how to decide by themselves, in the light of Christ's message, what is right and fitting and what is not. When men lived in a society held together by a tradition they were to a large extent moulded by the customs hallowed by that tradition. Whenever they defied custom and transgressed they were severely punished. But now the traditional structures and the restraints they imposed have in most places fallen away; man is thus thrown back on himself and finds himself alone with the decisions his own conscience has dictated.

That does not make for ease of government. In the Church, as in the state, there are associations and pressure groups, charismatics and theologians to make life more difficult for those who have to shoulder final responsibility. However, the idea of freedom of conscience cannot now be erased from men's minds. It is no part of the duty of Church government to suppress those outpourings of the Spirit that spurt up from below; but there is certainly a duty to examine them in the light of the Spirit, give them due encouragement and allow them to interact with tradition in creative tension.

After all, there is only one choice open to us: either

we draw closer, through dialogue and sharing, to an ideal state of affairs corresponding fully to the dignity of man, or we finish up in chaos with no prospect except that of relapsing into totalitarian dictatorship. The age of freedom of conscience is upon us, inexorably.

We ought therefore to keep uppermost in our minds the thought of the immense potential, in ideas and energy, that can be released when decisions lie not with the parish priest or the superior alone but with the community together with him. What a model of wise use of freedom of conscience we could thus offer to the world.

III. The idea of theological pluralism

This stems directly from the two preceding ideas of the local Church and freedom of conscience. Although only one continent has until now produced theology — and even there only a small band of men, principally the mediaeval theologians and their successors — today there are theological faculties and periodicals in Latin America, Africa and Asia as well; above all there are lively communities there, reading and living the Gospel and thus doing theology existentially. So, mission in six continents and consequently theology in six continents too.

Once again I say that we must not look only at the risks but above all at the opportunities, and we must be very glad indeed that the Spirit should be so lavish with his gifts to the Church in our day.

IV. The idea of integral salvation

I am of the opinion that a proper understanding of integral salvation (salvation encompassing man's whole existence — see also VII, p. 72) is dependent on a new awareness of the most important way in which Christ is present to us. Hitherto it has been customary to lay great stress on the historical Christ, on how he lived, taught, died and rose again. He is still the foundation of our faith. Then, too, there is the glorified Christ, most evident in the Pantokrator of Byzantine religious art, and also the eucharistic Christ, thought of principally in terms of individual personal devotion to the Real Presence.

Today we are discovering the mystical Christ, present in the poor, the needy, the sick, those imprisoned or oppressed — all 'his brethren'. The bolder spirits of the second Vatican Council — Lercaro, Montini, Camara, Suenens — took that as their basic principle and so pointed the way for the 'Church of the poor', a concept far more easy to talk about than to put into practice.

Well now, one fundamental lesson taught by history is that when ideas fail to make their impact, physical violence comes to their aid. That is how it was with the French Revolution, that is how it was with the demise of the Church as a state, that is how it has been with the communist revolution. The socialist and communist ring is steadily closing in on the Church; and in many places the Church has no choice but to become indeed the Church of the poor, to give up all her privileges and share the life of the poor. But at the same time she can convey to the joyless communist world a touch of the Johannine spirituality — the spirit of St John the Apostle and Pope John, joy, peace and love. E. Cardenal wrote in his book on Cuba that Havana is a 'monastery city', that there the monk has no need to flee the world because there he is perfectly at home; yet there one finds no joy, no smiles, no relaxed serenity, no faith in the heavenly Father of the Gospel. We have good reason for surmising that the Gospel will be the most widely read book, at all levels, in the world that awaits us.

V.   The idea of ecumenism

Until recently we cultivated a niggardly exclusivism: we were the Church, the 'chosen people', and the others were heretics, schismatics and pagans. We now realise that more or less every people has considered itself the chosen people. For instance, a 17th century Italian Capuchin, A. Cavazzi, wrote in his chronicle of the Congo that the people there considered themselves the best and wisest in the world; when God created the world, they maintained, he gave the angels the job of beautifying the various countries but the Congo he reserved for himself . . .

In the meantime biblical studies have opened up a new way of approach to the Protestants, and the objective study of comparative religion has done the same for our relations with non-Christians. The movement is only just beginning, and there will be still more powerful surges that will breach many of the old fortifications. All the signs are that the different christian Churches will unite more and more at national level to form a sort of league of Churches, that all the christian Churches will be invited to the next Council — Vatican III or Jerusalem II — in order to re-establish unity on one basis or another, and that in Asia the liturgy will include readings not only from the Old Testament but also from the Koran and the Upanishad.

With openness like this, a genuine alternative to the Communist international can be offered: *oikumene*, fellowship, a world community corresponding both to the plan of God and to the real good of humanity, a foretaste of the eschatological community.

Conclusion

This acceptance of the 'modern' ideas does not mean that there is no longer a Catholic viewpoint or a Catholic identity. Our Church will be the vanguard of the great people of God, the guide that leads humanity towards God, the 'model' of the 'elect', endowed with the fulness of the word of God and of the sacraments.

She will no longer be tempted to set up an ideal state by force of law and legal sanctions, or to impose a uniform type of christianity, or to prove her own pre-eminence on the basis of documentary evidence, or to struggle to defend her own privileges.

She will live the life of the Gospel in simplicity and exemplary fidelity; she will try to make that life accessible and credible, and will try in this way always and untiringly to act as a stimulus to the other Churches and the other religions. Above all she will believe with unshakeable faith that the risen Lord and his Spirit are with her. Thus she will succeed in finding a meaning hidden behind all the apparent absurdity of life, and in giving not only a new dimension to history but a new hope to humanity.

By acting like this she will create an atmosphere of serenity and trustfulness. Amid all the general disillusionment and disorientation she will be the group of people who sing the alleluia and come to their neighbour's aid with both word and deed so as to reduce one another's material and spiritual need.

Then the others will say: "See how they love one another" and will feel a secret longing. That is how the Lord will "add to their community those destined to be saved" (Acts 2: 47).

Clearly, the future ahead for mission is by no means hopeless except in the eyes of those who mourn the good old days and follow them right down into their grave. But even they need not abandon hope, because their graves too will open and it will be Easter again. Then, like a new generation of Emmaus disciples, they will realise that all these things 'had to happen' and that it was thus that the Messiah was destined to enter into his glory, and we ourselves with him.

'CONVERSION' AND EVANGELISATION'S MEANING

One has only to look back over the ground covered by the missions in the last thirty years to realise that everything has undergone a radical change — milieux, men, methods, even the message itself. There was a time when the so-called 'objects' of mission were classed as 'primitives" 'savages' and 'pagans' (in the sense of idolaters) and when all mission work was geared to colonialism. The missionary — photographed more often than not wearing a beard and a tropical helmet and seated on a motor-cycle, with a rifle slung over his shoulder, a crowd of children or lepers around him and a makeshift wooden chapel in the background — still lived in his Victorian past, perfectly sure of what he was about. Christianity, being the religion of the white man, was held to be incontestably *the* religion for the world, and it set out determinedly to rout its adversaries, the non-christian religions.

All that has changed. Instead of the modest little chapels there are churches and cathedrals, instead of the schools here and there in the backwoods there are universities, instead of the small mobile clinics for the sick and the lepers there are great hospitals, instead of paganism we find religions rooted in the local cultures, instead of dealing with natives peopling colonies we have citizens of independent states and instead of mission stations we have local Churches. Quite often we find ourselves up against a very pronounced self-awareness — a natural reaction against the past — which in some places has gone so far as to demand expulsion of the white man and therefore of the missionary.

From being an all-rounder, the missionary has turned himself first into an educationalist, then into a development-aid specialist, and now into an advocate of total liberation and a promoter of integral salvation. No matter what he does he needs a sound basic training, regular refresher courses and an up-to-date ecumenical outlook; above all he must be able to adapt himself to fit in with the local Church in all sincerity and with intelligent sensitivity — essential if, being a foreigner, he is to be *persona grata*. Christianity no longer stakes any monopolistic claims but operates in a free-enterprise climate competing (though of course constituting a 'special case') with the other religions; and the only way in which it can prove itself to be the truth is by showing itself to be genuinely credible and capable of offering more profound experience of God.

In spite of all the conciliar theology describing the Church as 'missionary by her very nature' (AG 2, LG 1), these changed conditions have given rise to a missionary crisis in the western Church — a crisis still not yet resolved.

Do we have to see in all this nothing but loss and ruination? Ought we not rather to see that a radical transformation has taken place? Many forms and many methods have had their day. The message has been demythologised, and so has the messenger who was so sure of himself. But perhaps this has brought us closer to appreciating the real essential, the permanently valid affirmation that life as life — and therefore the lives of all men — was given a new meaning from the moment Christ entered into human history.

Set within such a context religion ceases to be

primarily something to be studied and learnt, a cult prac-
tised in a church building but having no application to
real life, and becomes something that strengthens and
upholds and fashions life itself. That something is the
knowledge that since Christ and because of Christ every
child is a Christ-child; that in every man, and especially
in the poor and the needy, I meet Christ; that every
poor and needy man ought to meet in me the understanding Saviour ready to assist him in deed and in truth;
that salvation history did not begin and end with the
Old and New Testaments but is still running its course
today; that Yahweh, therefore, 'the one who is present',
was present while the colonial peoples struggled for independence over the last thirty years, present as they aspired
to human dignity, present as he once was during the
Exodus from Egypt and the wanderings in the desert,
always ready to help 'his people' (who nowadays are every
people) regardless of their stubbornness and obstinacy.
But there is one difference. It lies in the fact that in the
meantime Yahweh has revealed himself in his Son, crucified and restored to life, who remains with us 'always
until the end of time' (Mt 28:20); and so Yahweh's
presence within history has not come to an end but rather
has been concretised and radicalised, thus making God
not simply the God *of* history but God *in* history.

When life is seen from this angle religion acquires
relevance. It ceases to be something mainly for school
children who are easily influenced and old people whose
thoughts turn more and more often to death, and becomes
something for men and women in the prime of life who
are makers of history. Such a view does not preclude
prayer and cultic practice; it presupposes them. But it
does mean that our prayer during the celebration of the
Eucharist ought not to be primarily and almost exclusively concerned with attaining 'the blessings of eternity',
as if God did not take man seriously in the here and now,
caring only about his immortal soul and not at all about
mortal man and his present-day history. Rather we should

87

first of all learn to open ourselves to the Spirit of Jesus in the readings from scripture, so as to be ready and willing, after sharing the eucharistic bread, to share our daily bread as well, thus doing 'in memory of him' the things done by him who laboured for all men and gave himself up to death for humanity's sake.

After all, the signs of the coming of the messianic kingdom are these: "The blind see, the lame walk, lepers are healed, the deaf hear, the dead are restored to life and the good news is proclaimed to the poor" (Mt 11:5) — in other words, better things are even now afoot. Only thus can we imbue with credibility our preaching that just as we are in God's hands in our lifetime so too will it be with us in death and after death. We cannot allow what has happened in many places to happen again: in many places we had been working for decades among a God-fearing people without ever getting anything decisive moving, when suddenly there appeared on the scene a crowd of youngsters and others who, using a maoist-inspired revolutionary technique, are now giving self-awareness to the masses by a process of 'conscientisation' ('dynamisation' if you prefer) and are fighting energetically against ignorance, sickness, lethargy, apathy, prostitution, discrimination, tribalism and alcoholism. If religion is incapable of seeing itself as meant to animate aspirations such as these, and if Christians do not take up positions in the forefront of these movements instead of constituting latent opposition to them, then religion's future prospects will be poor, and once again — and rightly — religion will be accused of being 'alienation' and 'the opium of the people'.

This being so, the great changes that have taken place over the last three decades, and the new ideas we have accepted in the last few years, should not be seen as loss but rather as gain, as a radical transformation, an escape from the ghetto, a beginning from which more can be hoped to flow, a form of mission that will be lasting as well as capable of overcoming the present crisis.

* * *

'Radical transformation' is an expression that not only sums up what has emerged from these latter years of missionary endeavour but also makes clear what has always lain at the very heart of mission — all that is meant by the biblical term 'conversion'. When Jesus first began his preaching he said: "Repent, for the kingdom of heaven is close at hand" (Mt 4:17), meaning: "Let this message make its mark on you, stop and think; then make a completely fresh start, with your whole life set on this new hope". In its biblical meaning this 'repentance' or 'conversion' is a radical decision taken once and for all. In the missions we still meet it in its classical form when an adult hears the message and says: "Yes; if that is how things stand, then I want to be a believer and be baptised", when Jesus's entry into a person's life is *the* great event — as was the case with the old man Simeon, with Peter and John and many other disciples at that time who met the Lord and bore the marks of that meeting for the rest of their lives. Those of us who were baptised in infancy, receiving conversion as a gift while we were still tiny, have no direct personal knowledge of this profound experience. Consequently we have to acquire it by taking numerous other decisions; we have to keep it ever fresh and we have to build it into the whole fabric of our spiritual lives.

Setting one's sights on the kingdom of God does not mean gaining possession of a thing of some kind but, rather, continually realising that the variously tempting offers the world makes to us are not what matters. It means searching, and then finding in Jesus's message an inner certainty that something is afoot in our lives, that this something emanates from a depth of mystery, that in Jesus God loves the world and that Jesus himself has revealed to us the ultimate mystery of the world's meaning — God; that the world is centred on him, that he is the source of a new creation and of that creation's growth towards perfection, and that while we await the coming of God's kingdom the liberating life-style of the sermon on the mount is — for us too — both plausible and possible.

It is impossible to reduce the coming of God's kingdom to one single all-purpose formula. This kingdom is something that wraps itself around us, embracing each one of us in the way best suited to our individual needs and expectations; yet it is always shrouded in mystery and can be perceived only by a kind of presentiment — and by faith. A film or a play can make us suddenly uncomfortably aware how mediocre a life we lead, and make us see that we too have bigger and better things to do. A negro spiritual may bring home to us that here we have no abiding city, and set us unexpectedly longing to set out for the fatherland, which is not this world. Faced with the wretchedness of a needy individual or of needy humanity, we may overcome our natural distaste and decide on some concrete action, as Francis of Assisi once did when he kissed the repulsive leper and in so doing found that what had seemed sour and bitter had become "sweetness for soul and body". One may perceive some deeper significance in the worries and irritations inseparable from one's responsible position in industry, politics or society, and may sense that in one's own small way one is a Moses with a duty to lead his people, the purpose being to advance salvation history in this day and age and to promote the spread of justice in this workaday world. A poor man can have an experience of God when someone gives him a chance to earn an honest living and support his family. A rich man on the other hand, lacking nothing yet often for that very reason a prey to emptiness and frustration, may sense that perhaps he ought to cultivate an inner detachment from his possessions and pleasures in order to win what matters. Finally the sinner — and which of us does not belong to that category? — will enjoy a sense of inner freedom when he finds a kindly confessor or takes part in a meaningful celebration of the Eucharist, and will be imbued with fresh courage to continue along this path and become more fully converted.

The kingdom of God comes to us in all these ways, and in thousands of others, in conformity with the boundless creativity of God's inspiration; yet it always comes in a way that opens our eyes, radically changes us, entails a fresh start and inspires fresh hope in life — a hope that exceeds human hope and often hopes against all hope. The kingdom of God . . . what a mystery it is! Mission is at its service, called to serve it. Forms, methods and environmental conditions can and must change, but the essence of what we preach remains unchanged. So long as mankind inhabits the earth men will secretly yearn for a fatherland, a salvation and a hope, for an absolute meaning to life, and will be grateful to those who testify to it all in ways that are credible.

It is not only single individuals but mission itself that must undergo 'conversion' and radically change. Mission should not lament the passing of the old forms and still cling to schools not yet nationalised, to white prestige not yet undermined, to doctrines not yet demythologised — in a word, to the good old days! It has to proclaim the faith to the world of today and the man of today, and that means a great deal more than simply teaching 250 truths from a catechism.

When the Lord assured the faltering Peter that he had prayed that his faith might not fail and that he might in his turn strengthen the faith of his brethren (Lk 22:32) he certainly did not intend to burden him with making perfectly sure that every catechism in the world (including those for small children) contained all the truths of the faith set out in the traditional formulas. What Peter had to do was help his brethren not to lose faith amid the trials of life, not to lose their way amid all the disorientation of humanity, but to put their trust in, and build on, the power of God at work in Jesus, to ground their whole existence in God, to allow God to be God and to persevere in all steadfastness with eyes fixed on his kingdom. With a faith like this the kingdom of God becomes an effective reality for the here and now, and already begins to transform this world into a paradise — until one day we shall see "a new heaven and a new earth" (Rev 21:1). Supported by such a faith, every missionary and every Christian can be an unfaltering Peter for his brethren.

*   *   *

The Church's mission is timeless. Yet today it is, in a new and ultimate sense, passing through a phase of transforming change occasioned by a switch-over in history that is ushering in the Third Church. What multiformity, what a theological, liturgical and christian springtime we can look forward to, thanks to the Church's presence in the world of the poor, young, dynamic coloured peoples! Those who until a short time ago were called 'barbarians' will bring about a new flowering comparable with that of the later middle ages, this time on a world scale and in the spirit of the third millennium.

Anyone who clings to outward forms (always a secondary consideration), who allows history a right to run its course only along lines drawn by the past and not by the future, who puts his faith exclusively in the Church in monolithic western guise, will lose his bearings and fall prey to panic on hearing talk of theological pluralism, greater autonomy for local Churches, incarnation of the christian message in the cultures (at last recognised as such) of the other continents. But anyone who completes the process of radical transformation and knows how to read the signs of the times will breathe a deep sigh of relief and thank God for being so powerful a force in the history of our time.

X

PASTORAL REFLECTIONS ON THE CHURCH IN SOCIALIST COUNTRIES

These reflections should be understood not in the context of countries which are hoping to build a fairer and more just society without resorting to communism but in the context of the many countries where the Church finds herself faced with a *fait accompli* and has to deal with governments that are socialist or communist. There is no ignoring the fact that in the three post-war decades the map of the world has changed out of all recognition, politically speaking, as decolonisation has progressed, or the fact that in the last three years it has changed colour, ideologically speaking, to a greater extent than we perhaps expected.

With the end of the Vietnam war three countries in south-east Asia at once succumbed to the communist advance. In Africa there are now at least fourteen states that have moved from the capitalist to the communist sphere of influence; some are partly christian-inspired (for instance, Tanzania, Zambia, Madagascar) but most are motivated by an inspiration that is marxist. Their number will probably increase, because they have clearly defined programmes and they come to one another's aid, as happened during the wars that were fought to liberate Mozambique and Angola.

Political realism requires the Church to look this new

situation in the face and ask herself what the outcome may be. As she herself said in *Gaudium et Spes*, "the joys and hopes, griefs and anxieties of the men of today" are her joys, her hopes, her griefs and her anxieties, because she lives in the world and "feels herself to be intimately bound up with mankind and its history" (GS 1).

I. The phenomenology of the socialist countries

Instead of generalising about the traits characteristic of the politics of socialist countries in the Third World (the traits appear to vary but basically they are the same everywhere) I propose to describe three countries in concrete terms.

(a) *China*. The 1949 victory of Mao Tse-Tung's communist army will perhaps go down in history more as a Lepanto, a Waterloo or a Leningrad than as one of those great victories that have changed the whole course of this planet's development. But for China it has led to four things. First and foremost: the Chinese people — 800 million of them, more than the populations of Africa and Latin America put together — proceeded to recover the dignity they had lost through the 'unequal treaties' imposed by the west. Second: the flow of the great rivers has been controlled, so the country is no longer subject to chronic flooding, the vast tracts of land now under cultivation have solved the problem of recurrent famine, and the greatly increased numbers of schools and clinics have rescued the people from their former pitiful existence — all this out of their own resources although at the cost of an appalling effort. Third: China has become a model for all the other poor countries, showing them how underdevelopment can be overcome. Fourth: the idea of permanent revolution provides a way of rendering harmless the ineradicable egoism of the strong (and of the bureaucracy, which always tends to create a new superior caste) — the way of one revolutionary wave after another. Obviously this model cannot be held up for imitation just as it is, because not all peoples are as hard-working, intelligent and disciplined as the Chinese and because the price paid has been so inordinately heavy. (It is said that anything from 1 to 16 million 'counter-revolutionaries' had to be crushed in order to produce a malleable population). A certain degree of limitation of freedom can naturally be tolerated — as in time of war; some countries do indeed live in conditions of such deprivation that only severe discipline can provide a remedy. Yet the much vaunted 'freedom' often entails abuse of freedom, benefits only the rich and dissolves into rank injustice.

(b) *Tanzania.* Here a believing Catholic, President Julius Nyerere, analysed the various *coups d'etat* occurring all over Africa and saw that in many countries the new ruling class had cared only for its own interests and not for the good of the people and had therefore been driven out by the army, the trade unions and other hopefuls and adventurers. So, beginning with the Arusha declaration of 1967, he has tried to make his country a model of socialism — a model midway between capitalism, which sets a man's personal sights on money-making, and communism, which imposes its own rigid system on him by force; a model intended to be based on spirituality and voluntary adherence and to offer all men the same opportunities for development. He has repeatedly begged the bishops and priests to help him, because the people pay attention to what they say: "You ought to be spending your energy not in denouncing communism but in helping me to build a society that has no need whatever of any type of communism. . . . I am offering the Church a new opportunity to identify herself with the poor, because it would be terrible if the communists were the only ones to espouse their cause". Yet one cannot in honesty say that the Church as a whole has come up to the President's expectations. It is principally the christian tribes (which thanks to the mission schools have bettered themselves and made money) that obstruct the politics of socialism and decline to forgo their own advantages in the interests of the poor. It could happen that Nyerere or a successor of his might be obliged to conclude that the principle of voluntary adherence is too ineffective, and therefore have recourse to stronger measures. That would be further evidence for the Church that nowadays the Gospel apparently no longer has any 'revolutionary impact'.

(c) *Mozambique*. Here President Samora Machel is trying to build a tightly-knit communist society. After centuries of immobilism under the Portuguese (who allowed the population to remain 80% illiterate) he is determined to make up for lost time, get the people on the move and fire them with enthusiasm to struggle for progress and human equality and against alcoholism, tribalism, egoism and prostitution. In evening classes the adults are being made literate, not only linguistically but politically as well; they are being dynamised, so as to make them realise that their poverty is unworthy of them and that by a communal effort they can overcome it. The constitution guarantees religious freedom, but religious organisations have of course had to adapt themselves to fit in with the state's laws (art. 33, 19). These laws are clear: the Church's schools, hospitals and social services have been nationalised. The Church as Church can no longer take any public initiative but she is left free to celebrate the liturgy on Sundays. The government is of course convinced that religion, christian no less than African, is nothing but superstition and that either it will die of its own accord or the population will have to be 'liberated' from it. Ideological confrontation thus seems inevitable.

II. The Church's thinking

Relations between Church and state, which in Europe have for the most part progressed beyond the mediæval phase, are starting to become one of the thorniest questions in the Third World. On the one hand it is perfectly understandable that the young states, like maturing adolescents, should seek their own identity, want to see it guaranteed and react hyper-sensitively against the missions which, because of their varied and highly-organised activity, gave the impression in many countries of being a state within the state. The young states now want to assume full responsibility and take full control of all that goes on in the country. On the other hand the Church, with her schools and hospitals, did perform a supplemental function which was useful for a long time. Yet her true mission lies at a deeper level, in the spiritual sphere. She can therefore move intelligently towards meeting the state's requirements and should try, as far as possible, to reach a good understanding with the state so as better to fulfil her own mission.

(a) First of all the Church has *something to learn* from the Socialist movements, and that something is unconditional commitment to justice. Certainly she has always defended justice in principle, but when socialism revolted against feudalism and primitive capitalism she sided for the most part with those in power. Also, in Latin America and Asia she built too many schools for the rich, and failed to understand that she ought to bring their children up to be socially committed adults. Didn't we perhaps make religion too much a *gnosis*, a system of truths to be learnt, rather than a thrust that transforms life and the world we live in? How is it that a thoroughly orthodox emperor, Haile Selassie, and the christian president of Kenya, both living in countries where deprivation is rife, joined the ranks of the richest men in the world? We ought to see in the communist flood a dispensation of Providence which helps us not only to refuse to accept certain situations but to become the 'Church of the poor', not just on paper in Council documents but in deed and truth.

(b) Then of course we also have *something to give*. First and foremost a more profound approach to the significance of history. Even if the communists are convinced that it is they who mould history while the Christians only make themselves dizzy with straining heavenwards, there is nowadays some realisation that whereas the communists need to leave room in their history for eschatology, Christians need to give anticipatory expression to their eschatology within history — if we are not to reach a point where the former preach a history without hope and the latter a hope without history.[1] During the 1975 international conference of 'Pro Mundi Vita' devoted to China, an attempt was made to analyse in depth what is now an established fact in world history. There was a belief that behind the quite extraordinary Chinese effort to overcome poverty it is possible to discern the God of history at work, and that just as once we talked of '*gesta Dei per Francos*' so now it is possible to talk of '*gesta Dei per Sinenses*'. And this fact of history might at the same time be a warning signal to the western nations who dominated the poor nations for so long but did not develop them sufficiently.[2] A similarly thoughtful interpretation was hazarded by President Nyerere during his third visit to Peking in 1974. In one of his speeches he declared that on each of his visits he found greater progress being made, yet at the same time he noticed a continuing lack of satisfaction with what had been achieved. There existed a will to give the people still greater prosperity and a life more worthy of men. Then he added this impressive remark: "I myself, as a Christian, see in your dissatisfaction a divine dissatisfaction". The communists naturally did not take this up, but perhaps they did a little thinking about the faith this man professed.

In addition we ought to offer loyal co-operation, not confining ourselves to accepting only what is inevitable and not giving only paper assent but collaborating actively. Aspirations towards progress and against discrimination, etc., motivate us too. When someone else makes more effective use of them than we do, we ought not to resent this but rejoice in it. In the first of his two letters Peter exhorted the Christians of Asia Minor not to shut themselves away from the pagans but to play their full part in the state as constituted, and to honour the emperor (a pagan) (1 P 2:11-17). In the socialist countries the Christians ought to be the best citizens and the animators of work in aid of progress. Only thus will they banish the old prejudice according to which religion is the opium of the people, an accusation for which pre-communist Russia, pre-communist Ethiopia and pre-communist Mozambique, etc., have provided the communists with ample supporting evidence. Only if she first demonstrates her unconditional loyalty can the Church later, at a suitable time, venture to be the state's critical conscience and give voice to prophetic protest, less in defence of her own rights than in support of the fundamental rights of men in general. It will always be the tragedy of history that no system is perfect, because the men behind the systems are never perfect. In spite of the best of intentions and the best of programmes, in the socialist countries there are forms of discrimination, rivalries and fresh injustices springing up that cry to heaven for vengeance. It is therefore all the more important that political revolution should be followed by Gospel revolution, to make better men of the citizens of the state.

This brings us to the third and decisive contribution. We must offer to those engaged in revolutionary activity a complementary spirituality; and we must offer it not only to the Christians — to help them to accept courageously the hardships revolution entails, and to go on smiling and rejoicing in spite of everything — but also to the most rabid and venomous Marxists. The fact is that man, whatever else is said about him, is not simply a factor in economics, and he will never be content with nothing but economic progress. He will always aspire to more distant horizons, will always be searching for a deeper meaning to his life, and will always in the end be grateful to those of his travelling companions who can give him a quiet word of hope when his need for it is greatest. P. P. Pasolini is certainly not the only case — though admittedly a classic case — that shows how a Marxist feels an interior emptiness, sees his life split between success and failure, finds this almost intolerable, time and again has to bid farewell to everything within a short time of achieving it, and finds no answer to his 'infernal nostalgia'.[3] For lives like this the words of Augustine should ring out loud and clear: "Man's heart is restless until it rests in God". In the field of ascetics we have nothing to teach the communists. But when it comes to joy and evangelical hope we do have something to offer them, provided that we offer it in credible fashion.

Many missionaries working in socialist countries are perfectly content to be relieved of the traditional 'works' and confronted with the choice either of integrating themselves completely with the life of the people and enjoying no privileges of any kind or of leaving the country. They are convinced that the Church there is living in an hour of grace, that she will be held steady by Holy Scripture and God's promise, and that as a live community she can become more than ever the leaven in the lump, salt of the earth and light of the world, as Christ willed that she should.

XI

DEEPER MISSIONARY AWARENESS
FOR TOMORROW

Are we chasing a mirage or are we on the track of a real possibility when we set out to deepen the Church's awareness of herself as a missionary Church with a duty to look to the future? If success eluded us in the past, when the presuppositions were all in mission's favour, how can we succeed now that future conditions are going to be more difficult?

Two things need to be said. Firstly: although missionary awareness in the past left something to be desired, it was nonetheless intense and widespread. How else can one explain the successes achieved by mission in the last few centuries and above all in the last few decades? Even if it is now the fashion, since Joseph Schmidlin, to write mission history in a critical, non-triumphalist vein, much remains to show us that a genuine missionary spirit has always been at work. The monumental history of Propaganda Fide, recently published under the title of *Memoria Rerum,* has 5000 pages of eloquent testimony to that.[1] Secondly: who is competent to declare that future conditions are going to be more difficult? They will certainly be different, but they may eventually prove to be more favourable as well. For the time being we are in no position to delineate them, and their delineation will in fact depend largely on what we ourselves do at this turning-point in history.

At first glance the changed situation naturally looks depressing. Enthusiasm for mission has clearly waned, suddenly and quite unexpectedly, since the second Vatican Council. There are still a few sheltered areas where the frost has not yet bitten off the flowers, but these 'friends of the missions' will not be able to support them for very much longer. In contrast with them the young, the Christians of tomorrow, show a lack of interest in mission that could degenerate into a total opting-out of all missionary endeavour.

Whatever the future may hold for us, we cannot ignore the fact that *one view of the world as mission field has ceased to be tenable.* By a process that is irreversible the missionary has lost the aura of heroism and romance he used to enjoy: this superman, who could turn his hand to anything and whom nothing ever dismayed as he communicated christianity and culture and sought to win the world to Christ, has been demythologised and shorn of glamour — much as the achievement of St Francis Xavier has been reassessed in the light of critical historiography.[2]

This irreversible process has affected much more than the image of the missionary. One geographical view of the world, a view familiar and dear to us, has ceased to be tenable. Until the second World War we Europeans felt ourselves to be the world's centre in the full sense of the term (cf. the maps on pages 86-87 of my book *The Coming of the Third Church,* Orbis Publications, 1976). It was Europe that called the tune in politics, in economics and in the universal Church. It was Europe that got things moving in the rest of the world, and nothing moved except in relation to Europe. Moreover christianity benefitted from the pre-eminence enjoyed by this continent of ours and was held to be indisputably *the* world religion.

Blow after blow has struck at this view of the world

and invalidated it. One need only recall a few of the more significant events of the last twenty years:

— Bandung 1955, where the Afro-Asian bloc was formed, signalled the beginning of political emancipation. All that has happened since then is already part of history; the end of the Portuguese empire has brought one chapter to a close.

— Paris 1956, where coloured writers and artists celebrated the spiritual epiphany of the black race, was the beginning of a spiritual emancipation.

— Algiers 1973, where the nations of the Third World decided (by collaborating more closely with one another) to break away from the world market price system, was the beginning of economic emancipation. The oil crisis very soon showed how much power had accrued to the formerly powerless. Who knows how soon the producers of sugar, coffee, cotton, copper and other raw materials may take similar measures — a dangerous boomerang effect produced by Europe's former arbitrary way of behaving?

— Kyoto 1970, where 340 representatives of ten different religions sat around a table to discuss religious problems they all had in common, was the beginning of religious emancipation — in the sense that Christians can now no longer claim as a matter of course to represent the one and only legitimate religion. The new prophetic understanding that God's salvific plan is worked out in the whole of human history is a fact of life that we can no longer dismiss.

— Lastly, Rome 1974, the Synod of bishops, was the beginning of ecclesial emancipation. Do not misunderstand me. The subject of local Churches had not been scheduled by the secretariat: it was meant to be studiously ignored. But the bishops of the Third World introduced it with vehemence into all the discussions. More authenticity, more freedom to decide matters of discipline within their own Churches, local liturgies, local theological

103

investigation, no more western tutelage, no more western-controlled missionary efforts — these few headings summarise the points they insistently made. For the first time the western Church had to recognise that the era of her dominance in the universal Church is at an end. About two-thirds of all the speeches were made by southern hemisphere bishops, Third Church bishops. Not for nothing did Cardinal Höffner afterwards say that the Synod had been a lesson in humility for the western Church.

There is no need at all for us to contemplate the sort of radical reaction the Protestants have in mind when they talk of declaring a moratorium — the return home of all missionaries and the suspension of all missionary funding for at least five years, so as to allow time for both parties involved to re-think their future relationship and so as to give the young Churches the chance to discover their own identity.[3] But the fact remains that the west has lost its world hegemony on the cultural, political and economic planes, and on the ecclesial and missionary plane as well. Add to this our painfully slow progress towards European unity, our impotence in the face of the problems of ageing populations, environmental pollution and the energy shortage, and our sudden realisation that progress has its limits, and we become aware that we are indeed going through a 'depression' phase and are beginning to see some of what Spengler was trying to convey some fifty years ago in his *Decline of the West*.

So, one view of the world as mission field has ceased to be tenable; one missionary epoch has come to an end. That does not mean that mission itself is, quite simply, at an end. We have already seen other empires crumble, other world views invalidated. We need only think of Germany in 1945 and then look at her subsequent rebirth; or think how the biblical world view has fared. Today we are no longer rash enough to take at their face value the stories of the Fall and the Flood, the descriptions of heaven, purgatory and hell, the bodily resurrection of all the dead from the Stone Age to the Atomic Age, as we still calmly did only twenty or so years ago. All that has been demythologised; but it has not been absolutely demolished. We have learnt to distinguish between 'literary embellishment' and the 'reality understood and affirmed', to safeguard the substance of the faith by reinterpreting it and thus giving it greater force. We must do much the same thing for the image of the missionary to the world. What we need above all is a creative pause.

But one does not get out of a blind alley by taking one's ease in a sheltered corner of it. Nor is it any use imitating the ostrich, even if this is the way our ecclesiastical administrators behave all too often, letting their daily chores absorb all their energies, not realising — and not wanting to realise — that the old order is no more and so making no genuine effort to draw up a new plan of action.

I believe that the only right approach to adopt is what I would call the Emmaus reaction: after the collapse of one's expectations, after one's rude awakening from the messianic dream, one should entrust oneself completely to Jesus and his Spirit, re-read 'scripture', that is to say history past and present, interpret it prophetically and recognise that all these things 'had to' happen so that a new door might be opened to the glory of God's kingdom. Then our hearts will again begin to burn within us, and instead of remaining paralysed we shall wing our way through the world of tomorrow proclaiming the message the Lord has given us.

Until now mission has allowed itself to be carried along on the tide of the times. (I do not of course discount its higher motives or overlook its bolder efforts). It followed the paths trodden by each rising empire and it enjoyed the support of the colonising will of the homeland. The missionary's reward was the knowledge that he was doing fine work, the experience of exercising great responsibility, the satisfaction brought by statistics registering success. All that is changed. What remains, and what

105

still provides support, is spirituality, faith, quiet certainty in the middle of the dark night of the soul. This does not merely help us to plod on in an earthbound sort of way; it at once creates a climate of serenity and trust in which genuine inspirations and initiatives are the only ones to flourish. Above all, if our pause is to be indeed a creative one, we need the creator Spirit who brought order out of chaos not only once but still does so time and again.

The first adjustment to be made, with the help of the Spirit, is in our thinking with regard to our position within the whole of creation and the whole of history. We have been too full of our own importance. We thought of ourselves as the 'elect', and we thought of Europe as the zenith, the centre, the alpha and omega of world history. The new textbooks of history of the universe (*Sæculum Weltgeschichte; Historia mundi*) now cut us down to size, beginning as they do with the first centres of higher culture in Mesopotamia, the Nile and Indus valleys and the valley of the Yellow River, the Polynesian islands and Central America, and only then — as if dealing with phenomena of secondary importance — proceeding to record the eastern and western Mediterranean cultures and finally arriving at European history. So our narrow horizon is unexpectedly broadened. We discover not only a greater depth of history behind us but also vaster stretches around us and ahead of us. All this has a liberating effect; it enriches us and makes our journey through life more interesting. We come closer to reality and we begin to create the genuine humanism of the coming third millennium, no longer perfectly content in the sheltered waters of our græco-roman culture but gazing in astonishment at the ocean-wide range of cultures outside it. Then we come to see ourselves as part of a whole; so we stop bemoaning the loss of our privileged position and rejoice as we set about the task ahead, knowing that all stand or fall, grow or wither, together. We recognise that all that happened between Bandung 1955 and Rome 1974 'had to' happen, that Europe 'had to' lose its hegemony in order to pave the way for a greater world and a greater Church and in order to accommodate that brotherhood of all mankind which we hope for and must work for since it accords with God's plan for humanity.

The Spirit also helps us to experience the dynamic thrust of genuine faith. We cannot have things both ways. The moment of truth has come. We now have to decide whether mission can stand on its own feet without the crutches supplied by colonialism, whether we are capable of finding the authentic reality of mission, whether we really take the Christ-event seriously, whether we still accept — in spite of the success enjoyed by present-day humanist philosophies and in spite of the challenges posed by the other world religions — that christianity provides a discriminatory element (not in the sense of something that excludes, but in the sense of something unique — as Hans Küng has described it in *On Being a Christian*). Then it will become clear whether we are going to be capable of offering an alternative to the total absurdity that so torments modern man even in the Third World, whether we are going to be able to give sense and meaning — through the cross and resurrection of Christ — to what appears meaningless and senseless. There is no need for us to spring to the unconditional defence of academic doctrinal systems as indispensable compendia of christianity. But we must, this being our duty, continue to proclaim to the world all that God has revealed through the prophets and through his Son to be light and meaning in our lives. Christ having conveyed to us all that he had received from the Father, man no longer has to start all by himself right from the very beginning to find answers to the decisive questions life poses.

If we no longer see our mission as clearly as we would like, that is because we no longer practice recollection as often as we ought. Recollection and mission go hand-in-hand, as Protestantism says. The same Spirit motivates both. The classic instance of this very close union of recollection and mission is found in Acts 13 which describes how the christian community in Antioch, while praying and fasting, realised that its two best teachers were being called by the Spirit to undertake missionary work. If nowadays we have a missions crisis on our hands, we ought to seek its causes less in the external changes the world has undergone than in a 'crisis of recollection' proper to ourselves. That is where we have to begin; if we don't, no amount of activity of other kinds will be any use.

A renewal of faith is of course not totally dependent on the efforts we may make; it is the work of the Holy Spirit who can and in fact does come and renew the face of the earth in ways that are undreamed-of, newly creative, abounding with life and freedom. Have we not already seen how, after the 'death of God' theology, secularisation and autonomous space-age man, there has been an instinctive reaction giving rise to post-industrial man, unreasoning spontaneity, escape into the mysterious, word of God communities, the *Feast of Fools* (H. Cox), the Taizé youth rally, the evangelicals' congress at Lausanne in 1974, the pentecostals' congress in Rome in 1975? All these movements produce individuals who are not ashamed of the Gospel (Rm 1:16) but live it and proclaim it far and wide![4] The 1974 Synod of bishops included among the most promising signs of the times this new thirst for prayer, scripture reading and experience of the Holy Spirit. All this inspires fresh confidence amid the prevailing gloom and depression. Those who decline to play any part in it are quite simply left to stand still, until such time as the Spirit may set them moving again.

In any event mission goes on, mission in a new form, mission in six continents, mission as the Church present everywhere among nations that are poor, coloured, young and dynamic, mission as the message of total liberation, total salvation — in short, mission as the visible sign of God's love for all men!

Lastly the Spirit helps us to recognise the new reality of the Church. Until recently Europe and America were Church and Africa and Asia were mission territory. We can certainly claim to have mothered the young Churches, just as Paul reminded the Church at Corinth that it was he who had fathered it in Christ Jesus by preaching the Gospel (1 Cor 4: 15). But these children of ours in the faith have meanwhile grown up and now lay claim to maturity. The fact that in 1952 there were only two native bishops in Africa whereas by 1973 there were 170 (corresponding figures for Asia being 31 and 144) is enough to show how unbelievably fruitful the last twenty years have been from the ecclesial angle. 'The end of the missions' — that is to say the end of a system whereby we provided missionaries, money and ideas and burdened ourselves with full responsibility for those missions — the end of that system is no bad thing; it is not a blow inflicted on Mother Church but, rather, the crowning achievement of our missionary activity. The spark ignited the fuel, the engine started up and it is still running. When the *Ius Commissionis* was revoked on February 24 1969, 'our missions' did not become a no-man's-land, nor did they fall into enemy hands; they became young and autonomous local Churches which now, for their part, are changing into new agents of evangelisation all over the world and especially in their own world. What an enrichment we can expect when it is no longer a case of one continent setting out on mission to the other five but of priests and laity in every continent living the Gospel and handing it on by their own best efforts!

Obviously these Churches are not so independent that they no longer need us at all. "No Church — western or other — is called by God to become independent. Rather they are all called to actualise their own unique and non-interchangeable identity, and to enrich one another by mutual exchange and aid, so as to co-operate more credibly and effectively in achieving humanity's full liberation within the framework of Christ's plan of salvation".[5] If one Church should claim to be totally independent, that would be nothing more nor less than presumptousness. *Koinonia*, communion, contact and communication are all part and parcel of the life and nature of every local Church.

For every local Church mission beyond the confines of its own territory is still a vital function, and it calls for co-responsibility and collaboration on the part of every member of that Church. Over and above the theological arguments that can be adduced, we can now show quite pragmatically that we are not at the end but at the beginning of a new and quite extraordinary missionary epoch, because we can speak of the hour having struck at one and the same time for Africa, Latin America and Asia, and can therefore say that we face a quite exceptional global call to actualise the mission of Christ in the world of today.[6]

So this creative pause enables us to see that the changed circumstances do not add up to less favourable preconditions but provide us with a fresh view of the world and of the Church, a liberating view that releases fresh energy. We would do well to bring this, and the challenge it offers, to the attention of those young Christians who shed no tears for the old missionary image of the world but have not yet discovered mission's permanent meaning and validity. They are tired of official wails about the perversity of our age, tired of official polemic about communion in the hand, inter-communion, admission to and distribution of communion in exceptional cases, and other similar matters. A Church that not only inspires belief in her mission but also plays her part effectively — courageously and prophetically, in word and in deed — in moulding the events of present-day history, such a Church can still arouse their interest; but so long as the Church goes on being concerned mainly with her own internal politics, contestation within the Church will increase, or — worse still — will end up by inducing boredom and silent walk-out. We can certainly hope to reduce contestation by showing more evangelising openness, by practising a more comprehensive 'foreign policy', by playing our full part in mission — Christ's mission which quite simply offers salvation to a world in need of it, salvation for the body and for the soul, for the present and for the future, for the whole of mankind.

We do, however, need the courage to *organise inter-Church aid*. The traditional *cooperatio missionalis* was a unilateral effort, a one-way traffic. Today we have to join the ranks of the whole people of God, no longer in command but on a new partnership basis, a basis of fellowship; we have to be attentive and flexible in order to discern what has to be done little by little, recognising what each Church needs and what each Church can give. In this way our 'missionary aid' will give way to a *'rendezvous du donner et du recevoir'* (L. Senghor), 'cross-culturation', inter-Church service, fertilisation, stimulus and mutual enrichment — and all this not for reasons of diplomacy but for the sake of real inter-dependence!

Let us stop pretending we have everything to give and nothing to receive. Latin America is far ahead of us in liberation theology, in concrete commitment to human dignity, in applying eucharistic bread sharing to daily bread sharing, in Easter hope (negro spirituals), in renewal of the Church by means of *groupements de base*. Africa should excite our envy with her spontaneity, her *joie de vivre*, her untroubled faith, her outlying Church communities lacking priests but buzzing with activity — communities which could serve as models for us in the days to come when we too will be short of priests. From Asia we have already borrowed meditation techniques, and it is to be hoped that we shall soon learn — even from maoist China — the techniques of arousing awareness; for we have to admit, shamefacedly, that maoist ideology has been successful in getting mass movements under way thanks to animators who set the people on their feet in countries where for decades we worked among people who were simply 'devout' (Mozambique, Ethiopia, etc.).

If we at last see ourselves as the needy ones to whom others have much to give, then we shall once again be able to give without humiliating those to whom we give. What they hope for from us is something far more subtle, and far more important to them, than any material aid or tangible personal assistance: they want fellowship (neighbourliness, sharing, *mea res agitur!*), sympathy, understanding, acceptance as men like us, as the brothers they in fact are, tolerance and not condemnation because power has gone to the heads of some of their heads of state, time in which to fashion their own history — just as we needed time for ours and to this day are still a long way from being models of christian, political and economic virtue. The best possible missionary service achieves very little (like a heavy shower unable to penetrate sun-baked earth) unless the ground has first been prepared by this type of fellowship. That is why our top priority must be to cultivate missionary awareness, consciousness of one's own responsibility and world solidarity.

With an approach like this we can give the young local Churches the necessary confidence in themselves. We are to stop mothering them. They ought not to become colourless copies of our western Church. Let us set the young birds free to fly; they will find their way by themselves. The creator Spirit who has given migratory birds the necessary instinct will not fail to give the young Churches the necessary inspiration and inner maturity. We have reached an historical turning-point similar to the one reached when the Church of the Hebrews became the Church of the Gentiles. For 2000 years the Church has been qualitatively and quantitatively the Church of the west; she is now on the point of becoming the Church of the world. But she must be ready to pay the price of this by de-westernising herself and abandoning all monopolistic claims in favour of western ecclesial forms. We must not load the Churches of the other continents with the full weight of western tradition, for they possess their own self-understanding — political, cultural and ecclesial. They want to incarnate the Gospel in their own cultures, giving it flesh of their flesh, spirit of their spirit.

Much has been said as a matter of principle, and much has been clearly expressed in Council and Synod documents, about a multiplicity of forms being quite compatible with unity of faith. But when opportunity offers, all this is retracted 'for love of the unique Church and the unique Pastor'; a better way of saying it would be 'for fear of having to make changes affecting an ecclesial uniformity that is based on contingent European history and disciplinary rules'. The tug-of-war that began during the 1974 Synod on this subject dear to the local Churches did not come to an end with the end of that Synod.

There was a time when the western Church used to impose on the missions the old abstract anti-Reformation catechism, but the harm this did was rectified by the Council. We now live in a Church that is more in keeping with the Gospel, a Church worthy of being offered to the world. Besides renewal, which is still far from complete, it seems to me that the most urgent task for the theologians at present is that of studying in greater depth the whole complex of subjects related to local Churches and pluralism, untiringly debating it more and more openly and insistently until a way is found of giving practical application to a theological balance between Vatican I and Vatican II, between universal Church with her primate and local Churches with their bishops.

In my opinion the pluralism we can expect is not something to be afraid of but something that will exceed all our hopes. Surely we can look forward to great things when Europe ceases to be the sole arbiter of liturgical forms for every continent, when a few westerners cease to be the only pace-setters in theology and when ordinary Christians in six continents will be reading, living and carrying into their own spiritual environment the message of the Gospel. The result will be a kaleidoscope of theologies in which the same basic colours will appear in constantly changing blends. It will be a theological springtime and blossom-time over all the earth. We are living in a fascinating age, and the task of deepening missionary awareness is potentially a far more rewarding one than many of those of 'the good old days'.

One more word about tangible aid in the shape of people and money. It is no use calmly going on pouring out the same sort of propaganda as twenty years ago and believing that to be the way to overcome the missionary crisis once and for all. Appeals strike an answering chord only when they are launched in a suitable political, psychological and ecclesial context. We must not close our eyes to the fact that a number of states have expelled the missionaries and that others can be expected to do likewise. We must not gloss over the fact that in some places the native bishops (notwithstanding their declarations to the contrary) and the native clergy are no longer keen to see new missionaries arriving. We must not hide the fact that to go on sending missionaries will not solve the young local Churches' basic problems but will merely postpone solution of them. Local solutions have to be found first, through an extended range of ministries and more emphasis on the co-responsibility of the laity.

Nonetheless there is still a need for missionaries. Although Europe, supposedly poor in priests, has 9.8 priests to every 10,000 Catholics and North America has 12.6, Asia has only 4.7, Africa only 4.3 and Latin America only 1.8; if the 2.2 milliard non-Christians in 1965 are going to be 4.2 milliard in the year 2000, nobody can seriously affirm, given these stark figures, that there is no longer any need for missionaries. Naturally they will have to be nimble and companionable, able to immerse themselves in the local Churches and so avoid the 'moratorium' reaction as a solution to conflicts unresolved. They will have to adopt up-to-date methods and attitudes of mind and live among the non-Christians as the vanguard leading all religious-minded men along the way to the Father. They will have to be messengers from the old Church to the young Churches, the sign and guarantee of the unity and universality of the Church, models of deliberate relinquishment of family and homeland, stepping over all frontiers for love of the kingdom of God just as Christ stepped out of his heavenly existence in the being of God in order to have an earthly existence 'for us' and 'with us'.

The question of money, too, must be handled in an up-to-date context. It really is deplorable that in the past mission was so closely associated in people's minds with money: mere mention of the word mission used to make the good Christian believe he must at once dive into his pocket in order to live at peace with his conscience. We also have to admit that our money led to the growth of christian communities that were passive, sometimes grasping and often ungrateful, or at least (as Bernard Nkuissi of Cameroon said) to Churches that were like gravely ill men kept alive by artificial feeding and repeated blood transfusions — in the shape of our repeated injections of money.

Nonetheless there is still a need for money too. But financial assistance nowadays must aim above all at creating the preconditions for a Church that can be self-supporting, at laying the foundations for all kinds of improvements (*Ecclesiæ Sanctæ* III/8), at raising the economic level of the country so as to enable the native Christians to finance their own Church. Any monetary aid that in fact impedes progress towards this should be withdrawn.

As for how the necessary money is raised, changes are occurring here too. In the first place, the system of bilateral aid is giving way to a system of multilateral aid. The missionary institutes, which in the past were the principal channels through which money reached the missions, have handed 'their' missions over to the local Churches. Fund-raising is now more and more in the hands of much bigger institutions such as Misereor, Adveniat and above all the Pontifical Mission Aid organisations (P.O.M.). These last have a great opportunity, but they must make their impact not by citing their impeccable documentary credentials but by showing themselves to be both approachable and efficient. The present-day need for a co-ordinating and compensatory body is obvious. An effort at long-term planning, perhaps involving on-the-spot work by ecclesiastical finance experts, could result in plans for regional financing; this would help episcopal conferences favouring the idea to get their finances on a sound and equitable footing before too long.

Secondly, alms-gathering is giving way to inter-Church servicing. All honour to the almsgivers. But it is not right that the 'supremely great and sacred duty of the Church' (AG 29) should be forced to exist on alms-giving alone. Nor is it good for the young Churches to have their bishops travelling abroad for months on alms-gathering tours. In these days of 'socialisation' the Church too ought to find organic ways of meeting her own needs. The duty of all christian communities to pay a 'quota' — as requested in *Ad Gentes* 38 and the Motu Proprio *Ecclesiæ Sanctæ* III/18, and specified as 1% of parish and diocesan budgets by Propaganda Fide — ought to be obvious. The young are no doubt ready to act as pressure groups to get this idea adopted; they certainly find this solution preferable to the traditional small-change collections for the missions.

This chapter has set out just a few thoughts about how we can deepen missionary awareness for tomorrow's world. Precisely how mission will work out in practice in that world we do not know and we do not need to know. All we know is that the basic theological ideas of Vatican II — the idea of local Churches and the idea of freedom of conscience — are having the effect of delayed action bombs, and all their energy has not yet been released. We can and must prepare ourselves for many other things yet. Along this road towards an uncharted future, all the more interesting for that, we need only remain alert to the promptings of the Spirit, like Paul; that is to say we must pay attention to the signs of the times, find a prophetic understanding and interpretation of history-in-the-making and also set out trustingly to collaborate in the making of it.

XII

HUMAN HISTORY — A MYSTERY

To mark the 350th anniversary of its foundation Propaganda Fide has published *Memoria Rerum,* its own 3-volume history running to 5000 pages.[1] A work like this prompts several reflections.

While historians are grateful for the monumental *Memoria Rerum,* theologians cannot help seeing it as no more than the exterior of a building whose interior arouses their curiosity far more. In point of fact the gigantic commitments unremittingly pursued in the course of these 350 years — consultations, decisions, missionaries sent out, dioceses set up, conversions, baptisms — do indeed at first glance look like the outcome of purely human endeavour, in no way different from what is recorded in any other field of history. What is there, apart from a distinctive style, to tell us whether the subject is the tower of Babel or the basilica of St. Peter?

Behind, or better still *in* this exterior — the record of events as they have taken their course — the believer is able to discern a deeper reality. From his own experience and that of others he knows that in both the past and the present there exists a *mysterium iniquitatis*[2] (call it what you will — the devil, sin, inherited disposition, forces of the unconscious or the subconscious, or anything else), as well as the *mysterium gratiæ* which turns the confused history of humanity into a history of salvation and brings it, through times of light and times of darkness, to full eschatological completion. Unlike any mechanical closed system the Church does not contain within herself her entire *raison d'être* and all the factors in her development. It is the immanent and at the same time transcendent God, the God of history and of the *parousia,* who therein utters the first word and the last — the God who reveals himself as the hidden foundation and deepest meaning of the whole of history, and who enables the believer to perceive history to consist of a succession of divine interventions (*magnalia, mirabilia Dei*).

The conviction that all men and all nations are in God's hands, and that with 'mighty wonders' God effects his plan in and through historical events, dominated Old Testament and New Testament thought alike; and it continued to hold sway until the age of enlightenment gave birth to humanistic historiography. From then on history ceased to be regarded as history of salvation; world history and Church history were both demythologised and historians contented themselves with studying isolated subjects and devoting most of their energies to making accurate assessments of their sources. "The fact that 'Satan quietly disappeared from the scene of human history thanks to the pragmatic method' (W. Nigg) meant that ecclesiastical historiography as a special discipline became a narrowly factual exercise. It won scientific status, but in losing Satan it lost a name that had always stood very clearly for a reality that is over-simplistically set aside nowadays in all historiography: the reality of evil."[3]

Today however this humanistic conception of history is being countered by a revival of the historico-theological outlook, thanks to renewed consideration of biblical and patristic theology and hence of eschatological theology.[4] Starting from the fact that in the Incarnation God really did intervene in human history, an attempt is being made to 'break the Incarnation's monopoly' and to perceive God's salvific acts in operation everywhere and at all times.

Thus the Incarnation is seen as a starting-point, an exemplary model, a guarantee that the *magnalia Dei* will continue throughout the history of the Church and of humanity. In this way we have a bridge between the past and the future, and there is no gap in salvation history below that bridge. Jesus's first coming, meaning the past, and his continuing presence discernible by faith at every moment in the present together constitute the basis of our hope in his future return, and everything that occurs in the making of our history is geared to that return. Thus the believer finds past and future, history and prophecy, to be one indissoluble whole.[5]

Although there can be no shadow of doubt in the believer's mind about the validity of the salvation-history outlook on history, he must exercise caution in seeking to apply it in this secularist age. God's effective intervention in aid of his chosen people during war, famine and other catastrophes, placid talk of the heavenly Father who takes account of every sparrow that falls to the ground and of every hair of our heads, the many miracles attributed to the saints in the middle ages and since — none of these things any longer makes the slightest impression on present-day man, for he has learnt about the autonomy of terrestrial phenomena and experienced the brute facts of life. Anyway, God certainly does not sit at a remote-control panel, pushing buttons in prompt response to the appeals of men in need and so altering the course of events. After all that has happened at Auschwitz, Hiroshima and in the Gulag Archipelago — and still goes on happening — one no longer dares to speak of 'the divine providence'. It is typical of our times that God is predominantly thought of as 'absent' and that people experience difficulty in talking about God at all. Didn't Nietzsche say that a God who cured our colds and sheltered us from the rain would be rejected even if he ever existed? God is not our maid-of-all-work. A 'divine providence' of the kind many Christians still envisage is a stronger argument against God than any other argument imaginable.

'Providence' and 'salvation history' are religious categories, not natural science categories. It is impossible to demonstrate them physically, impossible to speak about them objectively; one can only testify to them out of one's own convictions and one's own experience, both of which can always be impugned by one's hearers. And doubts about individual instances can persist even when faith and christian hope are upheld by secure conviction in regard to history as a whole. So it is a question of interpretation and understanding by virtue of and in the light of faith. Just as it is with life after death, with Christ's presence in the Eucharist and with the supernatural efficacy of the sacraments — which cannot be demonstrated but only accepted in faith regardless of all negative appearances, and thus are bound up with trust and the fundamental option — so it is with the salvation-history meaning of history. God does not display the cards in his hand. And we are in no way competent to evaluate any one concrete event within his salvific plan. We are travelling along the way of salvation but we do not know exactly how far we have progressed. We know that the ship is making for a port, but we cannot pinpoint its position in the ocean at any given time. This is as true of the Church and of humanity as it is of any individual. Inability to recognise salvation in day to day events is part of carrying one's cross.

It is not to the learned and the clever but to the simple believers, those who have hearts that love, those 'mere children' of the Gospel, that the Father has revealed it (Mt 11:25), those who the Spirit declares to be truly the children of God (Rm 8:16) — that Spirit whose murmur we hear without knowing whence it comes nor where it goes (Jn 3:8); it is only these 'little ones' who can feel their way towards the mystery and sense the guiding hand of God both in their own lives and in the history (even present-day history!) of the Church and of the world. Blessed are those who can see this. Many have wanted to see it but have failed to do so. To some it is indeed granted to understand the mysteries of the kingdom of heaven, to others not . . . (Mt 13:10-17).

The essence of the apostles' *kerygma,* their message, proclaimed the resurrection of him who died, the presence of him who was absent and the word of him who was silent. There is no need for us to resort to supplementary interventions by the God of the 'beyond'. This mysterious God is present, as creator and redeemer, at the very heart of things and of men, and he guides and directs them while at the same time fully respecting their autonomy. Thus the believer is enabled to discover a meaning in events, a real meaning that makes them 'providential', one that in turn allows him to perceive with hindsight that in spite of everything his own life and the whole of history do have meaning. Anyone who achieves this, or continually strives to achieve it, makes a positive contribution not only to destroying the harsh concept of determinism but also to restoring to history something of the spontaneity and fruitful creativeness of God.[6]

So we can understand how W. Nigg was able to advance and justify a sort of '*amende honorable*' for the legends, and how, while the historicity of a given event can legitimately be questioned, historicity can never be made the sole criterion. An interpretation of an event in the light of faith, even if it is arrived at with the help of 'untrue' legends, is of far greater existential value than any pedestrian account of that event in a conventional historical record. "Alongside purely historical truth there is another more intimate, more sublime, more decisive truth. Truth exists above and around, before and after historical events. It is much more rich and potent, much more enlightening and breathtaking than anything that can possibly be contained in the straightforward horizontality of 'something that happened'."[7] As a postscript to *Memoria Rerum,* which is written with such scrupulous observance of historians' discipline, these considerations do merit our attention.

All that we have said does not apply only to Church

and mission history, which besides recording the direct, official and visible effects of the Christ-event discloses how one particular and unrepeatable history of salvation has evolved (albeit accessible only to the eye of faith). Nowadays we have renounced the exclusivism we clung to for too long, and we concede that the history of other religions and secular history too have salvation-history significance and value. The whole range of history, even though on a different plane, is co-extensive with the history of salvation and stretches out, consciously or unconsciously, towards eschatological convergence. It is the special function of the Church to interpret these deeper connections, to act in ways that will enable those who are part of non-christian and secular history to see 'all' historical truth — the truth grounded in the fact that, because of God's self-communication in Jesus Christ, mankind's position in relation to God is changed, and that this change and the newness it entails cannot be erased from the context of history.[8]

Naturally none of this means anything to the historian as a historian. His discipline obliges him to describe how events take their course, throw some light on the interplay of cause and effect, and say nothing beyond what his evidence can substantiate. Any historian who is also a believer has to decide for himself whether and to what extent his two distinct outlooks can merge. The answer will depend largely on the public he is addressing. There is no point in giving dogs what is holy or casting pearls before swine (Mt 7:6). In any case it is better to be cautious and reserved, especially in interpreting single events; otherwise words may later have to be eaten, as was the case with L. von Pastor who at first brought his 16-volume *History of the Popes* to a close with the tragic end of Pius VI and the apparent triumph of the Enlightenment, describing how the capital of Christendom fell into the hands of the revolution and how the supreme dignitaries of the Church were scattered to the four winds while the Pope's remains lay in unconsecrated ground, and then later — seeing Pius VII — found himself obliged to write a fresh ending, a triumphant one: "And yet the miracle has happened once again: the rock of Peter survives all storms throughout the centuries. The greatest, and the least understandable, thing about the history of the Church of Christ is the fact that the periods of her deepest humiliation are at the same time the periods of her greatest strength and most unshakeable solidity, that in her case death and the tomb are not signs of decline but symbols of resurrection, and that the catacombs of early times, like the present-day persecutions of Christians, can become her titles to glory".[9] However, that 'miracle' in its turn did not last long. Very soon Pius VII too was to be overwhelmed by a dark night and forced into exile for five years. . . .

So one must beware of singing victory songs too loudly. The triumph of good over evil will be assured and made manifest only when history comes to an end and the absolute future, which is in God's hands alone, begins.

It follows that in scholarly works there is no need to be continually pointing 'the moral of history'. All the same, the historian who is also a believer does no harm by declaring his belief and setting out his own interpretation of history in his introductory or final chapters. The time when religion was a private matter that never intruded on the political or scientific scene has come and gone. If the Marxists and other atheists have the courage to express their convictions, and if the non-Christians (Muslims, Hindus, etc.) look upon religion and the practice of it as an integral part of life, then the Christian must not blush to publicise his beliefs along with his knowledge and present those beliefs as an intelligent interpretation of world history.

From a retrospective review of mission histories written in the last few decades the following picture emerges. Schmidlin[10] and Mulders[11] stayed on the purely factual level. They were concerned only to offer "a complete panoramic of the subject, to assess the facts in a responsible manner, to throw documentary light on the causal links, discern logical sequence in the whole and give a clear exposition of the present state of historical research in the field of the missions".[12] No sign, no gesture pointing towards another possible approach to history. By contrast Delacroix [13] invited well-known personalities to comment, in prefaces and conclusions to each of his four volumes, on the facts narrated and to turn a higher light on them. So Cardinal C. Constantini interprets this history as a clear retrospective view of the great human-divine drama of the spread of the Church, one which today gives added strength to one's faith in Christ's final victory.[14] Cardinal Gerlier points out that the present-day missionary situation requires of the missionary a degree of self-abnegation that immediately makes one think of the dark night of the true mystics.[15] Cardinal Feltin is of the opinion that the great virtue of mission history is that it makes us see how the presence of its founder Jesus Christ is quietly confirmed and validated from age to age.[16] Cardinal Marella rounds the volumes off by asserting that after reading this history nobody unbiassed can entertain any doubts about the Church's future. There will always be people who respond to the challenge of love. The most important lesson to be drawn from mission history, which brings us face to face with so much generous service to Christ and his Church and so many extravagant demonstrations of heroism, is this: love is stronger than death![17]

The Protestant authors Groves and Latourette inserted similar comments within the text proper of their historical survey. Groves shows how the most recent missionary activity in Africa, despite a number of unfavourable background circumstances (the arrest and expulsion of missionaries during the two world wars, crisis in the inter-war period, etc.), has been able to develop in a very remarkable way. This, he says, is not "a new experience in the history of the christian Church but only another demonstration of the tenacity of the christian mission and the vitality of the Church which goes on growing in spite

of the clouds that thicken around it". And in his conclusion he emphasises that the survival of genuine
christianity depends not on organisation and intellectual
training but on personal loyalty to the living Lord. That
loyalty we derive ultimately from the Lord himself, from
him "who is able to strengthen you according to my
gospel and the preaching of Jesus Christ, according to the
revelation of the mystery which was kept hidden through
the ages but is now disclosed and made known — through
the prophetic writings, as the eternal God arranged — to
all nations so as to bring them to the obedience of faith".[18]

Latourette takes the same theme, developing it even
further, of progress in spite of difficulties because Jesus,
the Lord, is behind all this history. Every time the
Church has seemed to be on the point of dying, movements bringing revival have sprung into being; even when
things were at their lowest ebb there were signs of renewal
as these fresh waves formed. Indeed, in most instances
the Church overcame the crises thanks to a fresh commitment and a new missionary thrust. Latourette is wide-eyed
with delight at the tremendous vitality of christianity in
modern times, although when he was writing the last of
his seven volumes in 1944 ecumenism was only just beginning, local Churches were only just starting out on life
and the modern era with all its changes and possibilities
had barely arrived.[19] In a later work he sums up his
historico-theological thinking in the following sentence:
"There is much in mission history that defies explanation,
but nothing that can make christian hope vain or reduce
it to an illusion".[20]

Not only the histories of mission but also recent
standard works of universal world history assert that the
salvation-history interpretation of history cannot legitimately be excluded if history's meaning is to be safe-
guarded, that man is always in need of a *restauratio* going
far beyond his purely human nature, and that the
'enlightened' world still nourishes a secret nostalgia for
the traditions of the christian west.[21] It has been said that

the Church takes a pessimistic view of things, content to explain everything in terms of a fall from grace in consequence of sin as happened once upon a time in the earthly paradise, whereas the modern world is representative of the optimistic view which has unbounded faith in progress even though this faith has already received some hard knocks. History itself, therefore, demands *metanoia*, interior conversion: the nations must regard one another as God's thoughts in history, and therefore live peaceably alongside one another in tolerance and parity.[22]

The fact that a salvation-history interpretation can give us unshakable confidence in the future is no justification at all for the kind of triumphalist historiography, cultivated for far too long, which either allowed documents unfavourable to the popes and the Church to lie buried in dust or went to great lengths to embellish their contents. Since Vatican II even Catholics know that the Church clasps sinners to her bosom, that she is holy and at the same time always in need of purification, and that she must continually follow the way of penitence and renewal.[23] Indeed sin, with all its power over man and all the inhumanity it has displayed throughout history, is the right and proper background for the Church's saving mission. Just as the New Testament standpoint means that one must never talk about sin without at the same time talking about the Redeemer and his unfailing victorious grace, so it is impossible to preach about the Saviour without presupposing sin and treating it as a serious matter. The last word must always of course lie with the message of salvation. The Church was not sent into the world to issue reprimands and complain bitterly about the wickedness of the age but always and everywhere to proclaim the Lord's year of grace! (Lk 4:19).

Let us be quite clear on one point: the salvation we are talking about is salvation in hope! No matter how much progress the missionary Church makes in the world, converting men, helping them with education and *caritas* to live better lives and, being better men, to build a better world, no matter what form salvation takes for 'concrete' man who needs salvation in so many different forms, nonetheless the fundamental affirmation of Christianity is that so long as history lasts the world will never return to being earthly paradise or attain to being heaven upon earth. Salvation, in that it is an absolutely transcendental mystery, is to be awaited as something coming from God, not something at our own disposal. In the meantime those who seek salvation find themselves sent, quite literally, to work within secular history, the making of which goes on in obscurity and darkness; there they have to persevere, prove themselves, and retain their faith in the meaning of all things no matter how shrouded in mist that meaning may be. History will never be the scene of everlasting peace and uninterrupted light; the earth will always seem a place of death and shadow by comparison with man's absolute aspirations — aspirations which God inspires and which man therefore is in duty bound to promote.[24]

When J. Moltmann, after writing on the 'theology of hope', produced his new book entitled *The Crucified God*, he maintained that this was neither a step backwards from the clarion call of Easter nor a return to the mourning of Good Friday. If there is any truth in the assertion that the christian theology of hope emanates directly from the resurrection of 'him who was crucified', then the theology of the cross and the theology of hope are quite simply the two sides of one and the same coin. A theology that sees hope as the anticipation of God's future goes hand-in-hand with a mentality that puts up the necessary resistance amid the reality of the cross. Such a theology then helps to break the vicious circle of sin and to overcome poverty, violence and the absurd in life. Faith in the resurrection has no need to wait for death in order to become effective: it operates and shows itself for what it is even now — in this age in which we continually have to overcome lethargy and paralysing apathy and in which we have to shake awake our will to live and create a better world.[25]

The Church will ride the waves of history held erect by this hope of a better world but always keeping in view the world that has yet to know salvation. This is not to deny that there are some in the Church who consider that she ought, of her very nature, to keep her distance from the times, since those sailing alongside her will one day go to the bottom and the many cross-currents will die away of their own accord, leaving the Church alone surviving. While such a 'thesis' finds some support from history, it does not redound to the Church's credit but to her discredit. It cannot in any case be upheld from a theological standpoint because God is a God of history who always retains the initiative in saving his people through contemporary history (not through past history). Even to save herself the Church has no need to go into isolation; in order to save the world she needs to take up a position in the front line. This is especially true of her in her missionary role, for mission is the Church on the move; and it is doubly true at the present time when the breakneck pace at which events move causes the philosophers of culture to speak of an acceleration of history. At such a time the Church must abandon the philosophy of the static 'essence' and adopt that of the dynamic 'presence', just as we have ceased to regard the God of the Old Testament, Yahweh, as 'he who is' eternally and have come to understand him as 'he who is present' historically — walking with his people and effecting their salvation within history.

XIII

TOMORROW'S CHURCH AND
TOMORROW'S RELIGIOUS

This topic has to be approached with caution because the future is not within our power but in the hands of God. All the same we are not completely in the dark with regard to it. We ought not simply to allow it to rush at us like a hurricane, for there is much we can do to shape it according to our own ideas of it. We ought therefore to be asking ourselves, taking into account present tendencies and developments, what tomorrow's Church could be like.

I. Tomorrow's Church

Clearly, three outstanding present-day facts will have left their mark:

(a) *The fact of the Third Church.* Until recently our Church was a western Church. Her history evolved in the west; her theology, liturgy and discipline all developed against a western background. Numerically her centre of gravity lay in the west in spite of five centuries of missionary activity. So true is this that at the beginning of the present century 85% of all Christians lived in the west. But now, within our own lifetime, the centre of gravity is shifting and we can already estimate that towards the year 2000 only about 42% of all Christians will be living in the west while 58% — and about 70% of all Catholics — will be living in the southern hemisphere, in Latin America, Africa and Asia.

This Church of the Third World and also of the third millennium, the so-called Third Church, is creating many new situations for tomorrow's Church.[1]

(b) *The fact of local Churches*. Alongside the tendency towards universalism, towards a planet-wide culture and a world-wide brotherhood of nations, there is also very clearly a growing urge and will to live as part of an identifiable society, to preserve its characteristic traits and develop them, to experience the Church less as 'the Church the same the world over' than as an identifiable local Church brimming with its own life.

(c) *The fact of freedom of conscience*. In spite of all the risks it entails, this idea common to both present-day humanity and Vatican II can never again be erased from men's minds.

II. Tomorrow's religious

We no longer give placid credence to those who so exaggerate the glories of the religious life as to give the impression that inside the monastery all is salvation and outside all is nothing but worldly wickedness. Even the religious life has not been spared the general crisis. Even religious, who before seemed so sure of what they were about, now query their own identity. In one sense they have suffered devaluation while the people of God find their value enhanced. Nowadays there are undoubtedly members of the laity who live the Gospel in the world far more authentically than some religious live it in the cloister. Finally the numerous departures from both male and female communities have dispelled the glamour, the idea that in the 'state of perfection' all is perfect.

Nonetheless the specific function of religious within the

Church remains. The Council spoke grateful and encouraging words about them (LG 43-47; PC) and they therefore have to find their own role and carry out their own mission in tomorrow's Church. That entails:

(a) *Turning towards the Third Church*. The coming of the Third Church is *the* epoch-making event of current Church history; it is therefore a sign of the times to be taken very seriously. That means, on the one hand, that the religious institutes which in the past played 'a very important part in the evangelisation of the world' (AG 40) must continue to place all their best energies at the missionary Church's disposal, that besides giving the young Churches sympathy, understanding and assistance they must help the old Churches to rejuvenate themselves and overcome their internal crises by contacts and exchanges with the young Churches. The function of the religious orders and congregations, as international communities, is to broaden outlooks, emphasise the Church's universality and be the animators and co-ordinators of inter-Church aid in the young Churches (which are often tempted to a form of exclusivism that makes them see nobody's problems but their own). On the other hand, the religious orders and congregations are experiencing what the Church as a whole is experiencing — the shift of the centre of gravity towards the south. Many now locate most of their novitiates in Africa and Asia because most of their young recruits are coming from the south. One of their most urgent tasks is to invigorate those fresh entries, instil confidence into them and train them for taking over responsibility and control. It would be both depressing and useless to do nothing but bemoan the ageing process occurring in the west. We must rejoice in the fact that youth is coming forward in the Third Church, and hope that these youngsters will carry on the ideas of their founders and foundresses and continue, in the world of poverty, ignorance and sickness, to enact the role their institutes played when the west was in process of development.

(b) *Living within the local Church.* One must not be content to reside physically within the geographical area of a local Church; one must also breathe its spiritual air, taking an active part in it, living its life, giving and receiving in osmosis.

In the past some institutes lived in isolation, enclosed like quite separate communities. The 'holy rule', like the sabbath, stood higher in their scale of values than the needs of their neighbour. One's own holiness was the thing to be striven for. All that the common people saw of religious houses was an exterior behind which a life they neither knew nor understood wound its way.

Much has changed since, and thanks to, the Council. Religious have to put into practice within their own communities the *aggiornamento* of the universal Church, because these communities too are 'local Churches'. Then they have to make an active contribution of their own to renewal outside — within the ecclesial community, within the parish. Their contribution must no longer consist only of traditional 'works of mercy'; they have to radiate a new mentality attuned to the Council by exerting their influence in various milieux — small groups, conferences, schools, the liturgy — and by having many points of contact with all types of people.

This new mentality has as many shining facets as a kaleidoscope has colours and forms. One can do no more than outline it, indicating a few changes in outlook:

— from having to being: it is not what one possesses or lacks that decides whether one is rich or poor but what one is;

— from monarchical authority to collegiality, dialogue, sharing in policy-making and decision-taking processes;

— from meticulous observances of rules and regulations to personal fulfilment in response to evangelical insights, needs and impulses;

— from contentment with things as they are to an urge to pursue ideals;

— from a life of private prayer and personal holiness

to community prayer, singing and meditation, together with the people of God as well;

— from an ascesis of self-denial and small sacrifices to an ascesis of self-giving to others and a courageous commitment to justice;

— from a manichean outlook on the world to one that rejoices in nature, human nature as well as the inexhaustible beauty of the natural world;

— from a withdrawal from the world so as to seek God to contemplation of God in the world, in humanity and in history;

— from concern for the preservation of strict order ('*quieta non movere*') to hardy questioning, prophetic contestation in both Church and state, in the interests of building a better Church and a better world;

— from group egoism and provincialism within the religious orders to openness, concern for others, collaboration, oneness with the universal Church. . . .

To the extent that religious live and spread these attitudes of mind they will cease to be regarded as the watchdogs of tradition and will come to be looked upon as the vanguard of renewal, and then they can hope once again to attract disciples.

(c) *Acting as models of freedom of conscience*. Freedom of conscience is an inexorable reality. Dictatorial methods are no longer tolerated by men who have grown up and want to go their own way in freedom. This can lead to an ideal world, but it can also lead to chaos whenever that freedom is abused.

This is where the specific task of the religious orders comes in. By its more inward consecration to God, the religious life throws a bright light on the inner nature of the christian vocation and helps it to be better understood (cf. AG 18). In other words, religious are to set an example of how to put freedom of conscience into practice in life. They are not content with duly meeting the normal requirements of the christian life: in a gesture made in absolute freedom of choice they renounce three fundamental human rights — to own money, to marry and to go their own way — so as to be more fully available for the good of the kingdom of God, to orient their lives totally towards the definitive good and thus to give Christians and all men a credible sign of christian hope. Freedom of choice exercised in this way stimulates others, and prevents hope of a better world from becoming completely lost amid the criminality and moral decadence that surround our lives.

It goes without saying that, notwithstanding the Council, not all religious are 'models'. They too are simply on their way and so always in need of reform. They will best serve the Church not by drawing up beautifully renewed constitutions but by producing new faces and figures who will indeed be models capable of giving Christians a sight of heroism in everyday life. There is much to suggest that, by way of new situations such as those already existing in eastern Europe and other marxist states, history will help religious to become through and through what they ought to be. Unintentionally, and against their own will, such states do the Church a service, just as the Roman emperors did her a service by their persecutions which confronted Christians with the choice between apostasy and radical witness to the Gospel.

In this way religious, and Christians with them, reach out not only towards the future of the Church but beyond that future towards the age when history and its work are done, when freedom of conscience surrenders to enchantment with God and when there will be a new world that is indeed a state of salvation.

XIV

THE ENDURING MESSAGE OF
ST FRANCIS

Francis is relevant at all times and in all places, and continually surprises us with his freshness. The wonder he awakens in us is endless. His love of nature, of mankind and of God, his poverty and simplicity, his intuitions and his zeal in preaching the Gospel never cease to merit consideration and imitation.

Let us deal only with this last aspect of him. The way in which Francis always said "Peace and goodwill", the way in which he carried *shalom,* salvation everywhere, the way in which he 'evangelised' (to use modern parlance) — this is what gives his message validity even today. From among the many documents capable of illustrating the form taken by his evangelisation let us select his early 'unapproved' Rule; this — a mosaic of biblical texts which had struck him forcibly and which he wanted to pass on to his companions as the path they should tread — remains a perfect expression of the saint's original spirit. The later 'approved' Rule bears traces of the jurists' chiselling mentality.[1]

Francis's message can be summed up under five headings.

I. *The impulse*

After Christ and after Paul, Francis can perhaps be considered the greatest missionary pioneer in history. In saying this I do not in the least wish to detract from the greatness of St Francis Xavier and all the missionaries who travelled to other continents after the age of discovery. They, however, swam with the tide of their time and trod the paths cut by the colonial system.

But Francis swam against the tide of his time. Europe had by then become the christian west, but there was a danger that it would be content to perpetuate its own introverted existence. On the west it was hemmed in by the ocean and on the south and east by Islam. Nobody then gave a thought to mission — except Francis. An irresistible impulse urged him to go among the Saracens. His first attempt was frustrated by a storm that hurled him on to the coast of Dalmatia. On his second attempt, when he was trying to get to Morocco by land through Spain, he fell ill. His third attempt at last succeeded: he reached Egypt on a crusader ship and there, in evangelical simplicity, accomplished his master-stroke. Deaf to all advice to be prudent he left the camp clearly unarmed, walked across no-man's-land and entered the Sultan's camp. There he talked to him about the love of God and won his friendship. For the first time the Sultan had found a Christian who was not an enemy but a friend. Nowadays there are some specialists who say that the history of islamochristian relations could have been different if the example set by Francis had been followed by others. Francis was also the first founder of a religious order to insert a chapter on mission in the Rule, a chapter which had its effects immediately. Members of his order found their way as far as Tibet and Peking before the sea route was discovered. Where did this impulse come from?

Francis discloses his secret in the sixteenth chapter of the Rule when he speaks of the brothers "who by divine inspiration have the desire to go among the Saracens". Before this phrase he quotes the Lord's words: "Look, I am sending you . . .". So all is clear: it is the Lord who is sending the brothers among the Saracens and it was the Lord who spurred Francis himself to undertake his audacious actions. "By divine inspiration", in the Lord, in the Spirit, he had understood that the message of the Gospel could not be reserved for Christians only but had to be carried to all men, no matter what difficulties had to be overcome in the process.

Just as Paul at Troas was constrained by the Spirit, who prevented him from remaining in Asia and urged him towards new territory in Macedonia and Greece (Acts 16:6-10), so Francis too was open to the Spirit "by divine inspiration". It was from the Spirit that he received this impulse, which was far more potent than any present-day nuclear thrust.

II. The exodus

Fortified by this impulse Francis felt himself ready to "go out into the world" instead of withdrawing into his hermitage as he would inwardly have preferred. This is the guiding idea of chapters 14 to 17 of the Rule. In the repeated exhortations to go throughout the world we can hear unmistakable echoes of the Lord's command: "Go out into the whole world" (Mk 16:15). Francis did not found his community in order that his brethren might live a sedentary cloistered life, sheltered and well cared for in monasteries, but in order that they might go out into the world. He was the first to confront the most daunting aspect of that world — the Saracens; and he did it without any inhibitions. At that time christendom sent crusaders out *against* the Saracens: Francis sent his brethren out *among* the Saracens.

Intuitively he re-lived the biblical spirituality of the Exodus, which Vatican II has recently recommended once again to the whole Church.

Next Francis speaks of the preachers who are to go out into the world and proclaim the message of peace in the coming kingdom. For him all forms of the apostolate have to possess the missionary dynamic of outgoing movement. Even parish priests, hospital chaplains, prison chaplains, etc., must not be content with looking after the more or less good Christians in their immediate care but must go out to all others, not waiting for those others to come to them but setting out in search of the lost sheep.

III. Unity

Divine inspiration always operates in the interests of unity. In his Rule Francis proposes an ambitious synthesis between interior life and apostolate. The first thirteen chapters are concerned with the interior life, life according to the Gospel, the life of poverty — that is to say the life of vocation and preparation. But vocation and preparation for what? The answer is given in chapters 14 to 17 concerned with the apostolate. These are at the heart, the summit, of the entire Rule, and they are followed by sixteen further chapters dealing first with the governance of the order and then, again, with the interior life which must enfold all else.

Vocation in the biblical sense always has to do with mission. The prophets, the apostles, Mary, the people of Israel, the Church are all concrete examples of this. They were chosen not to constitute a privileged caste but to be sent to others. Francis wished it to be thus for his followers too. For him there was dual movement: 'going out of the world' in order to go out into it again in a different fashion.

We find another surprising synthesis, too — between the apostolate among the pagans and the apostolate in the homeland. In chapter 14 Francis speaks in general terms about this 'going out into the world'. Then in chapters 16 and 17 he distinguishes two specific forms of it, mentioning both brothers who want to go among the Saracens and brothers who are preachers. The close unity between the two types of apostolate should prevent any thought of competition from arising; and Francis exhorts all superiors never to hold back any who want to go among the Saracens on grounds of a scarcity of brothers. Anything of this kind would be a sign of "poor discernment", lack of ecclesial far-sightedness.

Unfortunately this wonderful unity is shattered in the later 'approved' Rule: here the preachers are spoken of in chapter 9 but the missionaries are relegated to chapter 12, which is placed at the end almost like an appendix. This led to mission being regarded for centuries as something additional, supplementary, of concern only to missionaries but not to the universal Church or the order as a whole. Vatican II and the recent *Evangelii nuntiandi* of December 8, 1975 have restored that unity and re-established the absolute priority to be given to the so-called 'first proclamation' to non-Christians.

IV. The activity

Insofar as it is possible to reduce the spontaneity of the Franciscan witness to formulæ, one can suggest:

(a) *Absolute priority: witness of life.* This in effect amounts quite simply to following in the footsteps of our Lord Jesus Christ (chap. 1), being present among the Saracens in 'the first way', that is to say living among men and serving them without engaging in disputation and without staking any claims (chap. 16). Hence the requirement that all the brothers must preach by their actions (chap. 17), both those who are officially preachers and those who are not, those who live in the homeland and those who live in mission territory.

Both the conciliar Decree on Missionary Activity and *Evangelii nuntiandi* have since given first priority, among the various aspects of evangelisation, to witness of life.

(b) *The specifically Franciscan element: poverty.* The historic Franciscan insistence on poverty is nowadays relativised. Francis was quite simply a follower of the Gospel and a precursor of Vatican II; for Vatican II, like Francis, has made the Gospel the basis of life once again. The community of the followers of Christ must live in poverty precisely because they are his followers. Francis merely understood this afresh in his own time, and lived it in radical fashion.

Poverty of this kind is not primarily something negative, not a renunciation, but the premiss for something very positive — perfect filial trust in the heavenly Father. The Old Testament had already spoken of God as a father. But Jesus did not just call him Father but used the form of endearment *Abba*, Daddy. By using this term Jesus brought about a revolution in human spirituality.[2] Francis took all this seriously, wanting to place himself and all his brethren in God's hands as fully trusting children.

That is why he sent his followers out into the world, as Jesus did, telling them to take with them neither money nor a purse, neither food nor a stick for the journey. They were to be content with whatever hospitality the people offered them (chap. 14) and see in it a sign of God's kindness, and wherever they met with rejection they were to enjoy 'perfect happiness' in abandoning themselves trustfully to God alone. When Francis sent the first of his brethren out on mission, despatching them to the unfriendly north, the only weapon he gave them was the quotation: "Cast your anxieties on the Lord and he will sustain you" (Ps 55:23; 1 P 5:7). Jesus himself echoed these words in the sermon on the mount (Mt 6:26). Are these attitudes idealistic and utopian? For the followers of Francis, and for all true Christians, these words are strength-giving, and they provide a guarantee that no realist philosophy and no human reckoning are capable of providing. Obviously this does not exempt us from the duty of taking normal human precautions, but reality itself makes sure that there will always be room for complete trust in the Father.

(c) *The real message: peace.* "When you enter a house, say: Peace be with this house" (chap. 14). In Italy the brothers are continually saying "Peace and goodwill". This can become a mere matter of form and thus fail in its purpose. Yet it can also be an expression of belief in the fact that in Christ we are offered peace, salvation, *'shalom'*, and that we therefore have a duty not only to speak the word 'peace' but also to carry peace to all men. Our entry into a house, our presence in that house ought to provide the people in it with existential experience of a peace that the world cannot give.

This peace mission can take various forms. Obviously it should first of all prevent the brethren from quarrelling among themselves (chap. 16). Then it should stop them from taking issue with anyone who offends them and eventually make them turn the other cheek (chap. 14). Then they will be amazed to find that "happy are the peacemakers" and that an 'army of peacemakers' (Helder Camara) does exist. Finally they must give to all who ask anything of them (chap. 14). Thus they can bring to other men some experience of the surprising kindness of God.

So the greeting "Peace and goodwill" acquires new weight and new content.

(d) *The thing we must not be ashamed to do: profess the faith.* Anyone who can talk of nothing but a crisis of faith and a crisis of mission, or who advocates nothing beyond simple dialogue and simple presence, finds no support for his views in Francis. In fact Francis speaks of a 'second way' of being present among the Saracens: the brothers must preach the word of God so that their hearers will believe in almighty God, the redeemer Son and the Holy Spirit, and be baptised and become Christians (chap. 16). And he adds this saying of the Lord's: "Whoever professes his faith in me before men . . . whoever disowns me . . . " (Mt 10:32). That puts an end to all discussion about whether mission still makes sense. Naturally Francis gives a criterion for judging when the time has come for passing from the first to the second way: when it seems to the brethren that God so wishes. These are very brave words. Francis presupposes that there are situations in which God himself does not wish preaching to be overt, in which the time, the *kairos,* is not yet ripe. *Gaudium et spes* would call this 'reading the signs of the times'. It entails discerning — in the times, in the events and situations occurring in the world, in the aspirations and hopes of mankind — what God's plan really is, and then acting accordingly.

(e) *The surprise: being prepared for martyrdom.* Unlike other leaders who seek to attract adherents with promises and pipe-dreams Francis, following Christ, held out to his missionaries and preachers the prospect of great discomfort in the immediate future, hostility on the part of enemies visible and invisible, and every kind of oppression and anxiety both physical and moral (chap. 16-17). Francis himself and many of his disciples set out on their missions with the secret hope of undergoing martyrdom.

Do we perhaps nowadays succumb all too easily to the temptation of seeing meaning only in self-fulfilment, of persevering only when things are going well, of hauling down the flag as soon as we run into difficulty or resistance, of giving in to discouragement, complaining of frustration, thinking of resigning? We must once again learn to take seriously the foolishness of the cross, go again to the school of the risen Lord who first had to be crucified, the school of Francis the saint in heaven who first had to endure the stigmata.

(f) *Dynamisation*

What Francis once did would be of no signficance if it failed to become a model for us to emulate. In the present-day climate of crisis — economic and political crisis, Church and missionary crisis — we need men who will swim against the tide, take action in all simplicity without a lot of 'ifs' and 'buts', hoping against hope. The charismatic activity of St Francis carries more weight than any theology. With activity of this kind it is possible to overcome the crisis in the Church, the defeatism of so many of her members. 'Divine inspiration' is still, to this day, a nuclear energy capable of breaking down all resistance.

The Franciscan movement is one of a number of movements owing their success to a basic idea, a conviction, a spirituality. In many other cases the ideas have won the day only with the help of physical force and violence, the French revolution and the marxist revolution being classic examples. It is up to us: either we take the Franciscan-evangelical values seriously and offer this alternative in credible fashion to men in search of values, or we allow other lay forces and movements to become indispensable to the realisation of men's aspirations — aspirations that the Church has not taken sufficiently seriously.

In his time Francis forestalled violence. He made it look silly, disarmed it with his evangelical simplicity, going fearlessly on his way in the face of opposition and danger — the way he believed he must tread 'by divine inspiration'. That is the enduring message he addresses to us.

SOURCES

I. — *The resurrection of Jesus and the future of the Church.* A lecture delivered during the second Settimana Teologica of Bari, 15-20 September 1975, published in *Aurora Serafica,* 47 (Bari, 1976), April, 10-12.

II. — *Elements of a fresh ecclesiology.* From a series of lectures delivered in various places in west Africa, central Africa and Greece.

III. — *Universal Church and local Churches.* (As for II).

IV. — *Initiation into prayer: its priority in catechesis.* A lecture to the intensive course in missiology, Pontifical Urban University, Rome, 13 February 1975.

V. — *Reflections on evangelisation and cultures.* A lecture delivered to the Episcopal Conference of Tanzania, Dar-es-Salaam, 18 November 1975.

VI. — *Evangelisation in present-day conflict-prone society.* A lecture to the fifteenth Settimana Teologica of Messina, 10-16 March 1975.

VII. — *Mission: its past and its present.* A lecture to the Settimana Missiologica of Bressanone, 22-26 September 1975; published in *Konferenzblatt für Theologie und Seelsorge,* 87 (Bressanone, 1976), 44-50.

VIII. — *Mission: its future.* (As for VII, 129-134).

IX. — *'Conversion' and evangelisation's meaning.* Epilogue of the book by W. Bühlmann, *Wandlung zum Wesentlichen,* Munster, Schwarzach, 1976.

X. — *Pastoral reflections on the Church in socialist countries.* (As for II).

XI. — *Deeper missionary awareness for tomorrow.* A lecture to the Catholic Missionary Council of Germany, Wurzburg, 12 June 1975, published in *Ordenskorrespondenz,* 17 (Cologne, 1976), 21-33.

XII. — *Human history — a mystery.* From the epilogue to S.C.P.F. *Memoria rerum,* Rome-Freiburg, Herder, III/2, 1976, 578-614.

XIII. — *Tomorrow's Church and tomorrow's religious.* Lecture given at various General Chapters and (expanded) to members of the Unione delle Curie Generalizie, Salesianum, Rome, 8-11 November 1976.

XIV. — *The enduring message of St Francis.* Lecture given during the conference on 'aggiornamento' of the Tuscan Province of Capuchins, 26-29 April 1976.

NOTES

Introduction
1. Cf. J. Feiner and M. Löhrer (ed.), *Mysterium salutis, Nuovo corso di dogmatica come teologia della storia della salvezza,* I-IX, Queriniana, Brescia, 1967-1973.
2. W. Bühlmann, *The Coming of the Third Church,* St. Paul Publications, Slough, 1976, and Orbis Books, New York, 1977.

I.
1. *Geschichte der Päpste,* XVI/3, Herder, Freiburg, 1933, 633
2. W. Kasper, *Jesus the Christ,* Burns and Oates, London, 1976.
3. K. Rahner, in *Handbuch der Pastoraltheologie,* Herder, Freiburg, 1964, 22.
4. D. Wiederkehr, *Perspektiven der Eschatologie,* Benziger, Einsiedeln, 1974, 56ff, 67ff.
5. J. Moltmann, *The Crucified God,* S.C.M. Press, London, 1974.

II.
1. *Brevior synopsis theologiæ ecclesiologia,* Paris, 1949.
2. H. Mühlen, *Die Erneuerung des christlichen Glaubens* Monaco, 1974.
3. Cf. E. Balducci, *Diario dell'esodo* 1960-1970, Vallecchi, Florence.
4. Cf. *Les quattre évangiles aux hommes d'aujourd'hui.*

III.
1. H. J. Pottmayer, *Unfehlbarkeit und Souveränität,* Magonza, 1975.
2. *Il complesso antiromano,* Queriniana, Brescia, 1975. Cf. also B. Papa, *Tensioni e unità della Chiesa. Ricerca storico-teologica negli Atti degli Apostoli,* Ecumenica Editrice, Bari, 1976.
3. M. Hay, *Failure in the Far East,* Wetteren, Belgium, 1956.
4. Rusconi, Milan, 1975.

IV.
1. *A New Pentecost?,* Darton, Longman and Todd, London, 1975.
2. Ann Arbor, Michigan, 1974.
3. Cf. W. Bühlmann, *Die christliche Terminologie,* Ed. NZM, Schöneck, 1950, 288-293.
4. B. Nyom, *Prière biblique et prière négro-africaine,* Lille, 1964.
5. *Das Gebet,* Monaco, 1921, 58.
6. AAS 1971, 692-704.

7. AAS 1973, 340-347.
8. B. Lupykx, *Culte chrétien en Afrique après Vatican II*, Ed. NZM, Immensee, 1975, 20ff, 88ff, 105ff.
9. *La terre africaine et ses religions*, Larousse, 1975, 333.

V.

1. A. Shorter, *African culture and the christian church: an introduction to social and pastoral anthropology*, J. Chapman, London, 1973; A. Shorter, *African christian theology. Adaptation or incarnation?*, J. Chapman, London, 1975; L. J. Luzbetak, *The Church and cultures: an allied anthropology for the religious worker*, Techny, 1970; *Les religions africaines comme source de valeurs de civilisation. Colloque de Cotonou*, 1970, Présence africaine, Paris, 1972; W. Bühlmann, *The Coming of the Third Church*, St Paul Publications, Slough, 1976, and Orbis Books, New York, 1977; *Eglise et 'authenticité' au Zaire*, PMV, Brussels, special note.
2. In R. Pierce Beaver, *The Gospel and Frontier Peoples*, South Pasadena, 1973, 79-95.
3. G. Gonus, *L'Eglise d'Afrique au Concile Vatican II*, NZM, Immensee, 1975, 46-50.
4. Agenzia Internazionale FIDES, Rome, November 16, 1974. For complete documentation cf. *Le nuove vie del Vangelo. I 63 contributi dei vescovi africani presenti al Sinodo del 1974*, EMI, Bologna, 1975, 350pp.
5. Cf. W. Bühlmann, *op. cit.* 372ff. For another explanation see T. Tshibangu, *Le propos d'une théologie africaine*, Kinshasa, 1974, 47pp.
6. Cf. E. Schillebeeckx,*The Understanding of Faith*, Sheed and Ward, London, 1974; C. Molari, *La fede e il suo linguaggio*, Cittadella Editrice, Assisi, 1975; J. Kerkhofs, *Principes heuristiques*, in *Pro Mundi Vita*, n. 54, Brussels, 1975, 7-11; P. Tillich, *Die religiöse Deutung der Gegenwart*, Stuttgart, 1968.
7. L. V. Thomas and R. Luneau, *La terre africaine et ses religions*, Larousse, 1975, 333.

VI.

Nil.

VII.

1. *Die Mission und Ausbreitung des Christentums in den ersten drei Jahrunderten*, Leipzig, 1923/4.
2. *A history of the expansion of christianity*, I-VII, New York, 1937-1945.

VIII.

1. *Mysterium salutis*, Benziger, Einsiedeln, IV/2, 430.
2. *A Cuba*, Cittadella Editrice, Assisi, 1974.

IX.

Nil.

X.

1. D. Wiederkehr, *Perspektiven der Eschatodogie,* Benziger, Zurich, 1974.
2. Pro Mundi Vita, *Le colloque de Louvain sur la Chine,* Brussels, 1975, no. 54; N. P. Moritzen and B. Willeke, *China — eine Herausforderung an die Kirchen,* Evangelischen Mission, Erlangen, 1975.
3. P. P. Pasolini, *La divina mimesis,* Einaudi, Torino, 1976.

XI.

1. J. Metzler (ed.), *S.C.P.F. Memoria Rerum 1622-1972,* Herder, Freiburg, 1971-1976, 3 vols.
2. Cf. A. Goodier, *Saints for sinners. The failure of St Francis Xavier,* London, 1936.
3. Special number of *International Review for Mission,* Geneva.
4. W. Bühlmann, *The Coming of the Third Church,* St Paul Publications, Slough, 1976, and Orbis Books, New York, 1977, 202-209.
5. J. Kerkhofs in *Zeitschrift fur Missionwissenschaft und Religionswissenschaft,* Münster, 1972, 167.
6. W. Bühlmann, *op. cit.,* 149-166.

XII.

1. Freiburg, Herder, 1971-1976.
2. 2 Ts 3:7 and relevant comments.
3. O. Köhler, *Die Geschichte der welt,* in *Saeculum Weltgeschichte VI,* Freiburg-Basilea-Vienna, 1971, 560-567, esp. 567.
4. On this whole question cf. R. Wittram, *Das Interesse an der Geschichte,* Gottingen, 1968, 136-150: "Geschichte der Kirche und Geschichte del Welt"; R. Schnackenburg-A. Darlapp, *Heilsgeschichte,* in *LThK* V, 148-156; J. Daniélou-A. Halder-H. Vorgrimmler, *Geschichtstheologie,* in *LThK* IV, 793-799. Question on the theology of history, cf. K. Rahner, "History of the world and salvation history", *Theological Investigations,* vol. V, 99-114, Darton, Longman and Todd, London; R.P. Milburn, *Early christian interpretation of history,* Black, London, 1954.
5. M. Schmaus, *Church, its origin and structure,* Sheed and Ward, London, 1972; Id., *Die Eschatologie* II, Monaco, 1970, 700.
6. Cf. H. Zahrnt, *Gott kan nicht sterben,* Monaco, 2 ed., 1970, esp. 18, 187, 224-235; M. Legaut, *Meine Ehrfahrung mit dem Glauben,* Freiburg, 5 ed., 1973, esp. 184-189; P. Berglar, *Geschick und Geschichte,* Darmstadt, 1972.

7. W. Nigg, *Unvergängliche Legende,* Zurich, 1964, 361-377, esp. 371.
8. Wittram, *op. cit.,* 31.
9. L. von Pastor, *Geschichte der Päpste,* XVI/3, Freiburg, 1933, 633.
10. J. Schmidlin, *Katholische Missionsgeschichte,* Steyl, 1924.
11. A. Mulders, *Missionsgeschichte,* Ratisbon, 1960.
12. Mulders, *op. cit.,* 7.
13. S. Delacroix, *Histoire universelle des missions catholiques* I-IV, Paris, 1956-1959.
14. *op. cit.,* I, 5ff.
15. *op. cit.,* III, 10.
16. *op. cit.,* IV, 11.
17. *op. cit.,* IV, 379.
18. C.P. Groves, *The planting of christianity in Africa,* IV, London, 1958, 194, 342, 356. The quotation is from Rm 16:25-26.
19. K.S. Latourette, *A history of the expansion of christianity,* I-VII, New York, 1937-1945, esp. 487, 504; III, 451.
20. Id., *Christianity in a revolutionary age,* I-V, New York, 1958-1962, V, 534. Cf. J. Kraus, *Missionsgeschichte als Heilsgeschichte. Zum Gedenken an K.S. Latourette,* in *Verbum SDV,* 12, Rome, 1971, 177-186.
21. Köhler, *op. cit.,* 560, 567, 569ff.
22. H. Steinacker, *Vom Sinn und Wesen der Geschichte,* in *Historia Mundi,* X, Berne-Monaco, 1971, 726, 730ff, 771ff.
23. *Lumen Gentium* 23.
24. Rahner, *op. cit.,* 99-114.
25. J. Moltmann, *The Crucified God,* S.C.M. Press, London, 1974; W. Bühlmann, *op. cit.,* 98-102. Cf. also the Apostolic Exhortation *Evangelii nuntiandi,* 1975.

XIII

1. Cf. W. Bühlmann, *The Coming of the Third Church,* St Paul Publications, Slough, 1976, and Orbis Books, New York, 1977.

XIV

1. Cf. D.L. Flood, *Die Regula non bullata der Minderbrüder,* Werl, 1967.
2. J. Jeremias, *Abba, Jésus et son Père,* Ed. du Seuil, Paris, 1972.

Also by Walbert Bühlmann . . .

THE COMING OF THE THIRD CHURCH

An Analysis of the Present and Future of the Church

"This is one of those rare books that quickly tempts an unwary reviewer to let his enthusiasm run away with his critical judgment. It excels in so many important ways that extravagant superlatives are apt to tumble spontaneously out of the typewriter.

"With fine scholarship, literary skill, measured daring and well founded hope, this experienced Capuchin missionary has sketched a challenging prospect of the Church in the next quarter century. It will be a time, he believes, of the flowering of new forms of Christianity among the peoples of black Africa, Latin America and South Asia.

"If you have time and money this year for only one serious book, *The Coming of the Third Church* is the one to purchase and study with an open mind and a sincere heart." *Priests USA*

"Not a systematic treatment of contemporary ecclesiology but a popular narrative analogous to Alvin Toffler's *Future Shock.*" *America*

"Karl Rahner called this the best book of the year, Sister Margaret Brennan, IHM, the book of the decade. It is both."
Sister Margaret Ellen Traxler, Commonweal

"Bühlmann gives some remarkable insights with respect to world population and Church presence; no author has dared to put the pieces together in the provocative way Bühlmann has done."
Pastoral Life

"When reviewing books for *Missionalia* I try to refrain from referring to any as 'required reading for everybody.' This book is an exception. I cannot but urge each and every one of our subscribers to read it, and to read it carefully." *Missionalia*

"A magnificent theological analysis of the contemporary missionary task." *The Christian Century*

ISBN 0-88344-069-5 CIP
ISBN 0-88344-070-9

Cloth $12.95
Paper $6.95

Other Orbis books . . .

THE MEANING OF MISSION

José Comblin

"This very readable book has made me think, and I feel it will be useful for anyone dealing with their Christian role of mission and evangelism." *New Review of Books and Religion*
ISBN 0-88344-304-X CIP   *Cloth $6.95*

THE GOSPEL OF PEACE AND JUSTICE

Catholic Social Teaching Since Pope John

Presented by Joseph Gremillion

"Especially valuable as a resource. The book brings together 22 documents containing the developing social teaching of the church from *Mater et Magistra* to Pope Paul's 1975 *Peace Day Message on Reconciliation*. I watched the intellectual excitement of students who used Gremillion's book in a justice and peace course I taught last summer, as they discovered a body of teaching on the issues they had defined as relevant. To read Gremillion's overview and prospectus, a meaty introductory essay of some 140 pages, is to be guided through the sea of social teaching by a remarkably adept navigator."

National Catholic Reporter

"An authoritative guide and study aid for concerned Catholics and others." *Library Journal*
ISBN 0-88344-165-9   *Cloth $15.95*
ISBN 0-88344-166-7   *Paper $8.95*

THEOLOGY IN THE AMERICAS

Papers of the 1975 Detroit Conference

Edited by Sergio Torres and John Eagleson

"A pathbreaking book from and about a pathbreaking theological conference, *Theology in the Americas* makes a major contribution to ecumenical theology, Christian social ethics and liberation movements in dialogue." *Fellowship*
ISBN 0-88344-479-8 CIP   *Cloth $12.95*
ISBN 0-88344-476-3   *Paper $5.95*

CHRISTIANS, POLITICS AND VIOLENT REVOLUTION

J.G. Davies

"Davies argues that violence and revolution are on the agenda the world presents to the Church and that consequently the Church must reflect on such problems. This is a first-rate presentation, with Davies examining the question from every conceivable angle."

National Catholic News Service

ISBN 0-88344-061-X   *Paper $4.95*

CHRISTIAN POLITICAL THEOLOGY A MARXIAN GUIDE

Joseph Petulla

"Petulla presents a fresh look at Marxian thought for the benefit of Catholic theologians in the light of the interest in this subject which was spurred by Vatican II, which saw the need for new relationships with men of all political positions." *Journal of Economic Literature*

ISBN 0-88344-060-1   *Paper $4.95*

THE NEW CREATION: MARXIST AND CHRISTIAN?

José María González-Ruiz

"A worthy book for lively discussion."

The New Review of Books and Religion

ISBN 0-88344-327-9 CIP   *Cloth $6.95*

CHRISTIANS AND SOCIALISM

Documentation of the Christians for Socialism Movement in Latin America

Edited by John Eagleson

"Compelling in its clear presentation of the issue of Christian commitment in a revolutionary world." *The Review of Books and Religion*

ISBN 0-88344-058-X   *Paper $4.95*

THE CHURCH AND
THIRD WORLD REVOLUTION

Pierre Bigo

"Heavily documented, provocative yet reasonable, this is a testament, demanding but impressive." *Publishers Weekly*

ISBN 0-88344-071-7 CIP   *Cloth $8.95*
ISBN 0-88344-072-5   *Paper $4.95*

WHY IS THE THIRD WORLD POOR?

Piero Gheddo

"An excellent handbook on the Christian understanding of the development process. Gheddo looks at both the internal and external causes of underdevelopment and how Christians can involve themselves in helping the third world." *Provident Book Finder*

ISBN 0-88344-757-6   *Paper $4.95*

POLITICS AND SOCIETY
IN THE THIRD WORLD

Jean-Yves Calvez

"This frank treatment of economic and cultural problems in developing nations suggests the need for constant multiple attacks on the many fronts that produce problems in the human situation."

The Christian Century
ISBN 0-88344-389-9   *Cloth $6.95*

A THEOLOGY OF LIBERATION

Gustavo Gutiérrez

"The movement's most influential text." *Time*

"The most complete presentation thus far available to English readers of the provocative theology emerging from the Latin American Church." *Theological Studies*

"North Americans as well as Latin Americans will find so many challenges and daring insights that they will, I suggest, rate this book one of the best of its kind ever written." *America*

ISBN 0-88344-477-1   *Cloth $7.95*
ISBN 0-88344-478-X   *Paper $4.95*

THEOLOGY FOR A NOMAD CHURCH

Hugo Assmann

"A new challenge to contemporary theology which attempts to show that the theology of liberation is not just a fad, but a new political dimension which touches every aspect of Christian existence."

Publishers Weekly

ISBN 0-88344-493-3   *Cloth $7.95*
ISBN 0-88344-494-1   *Paper $4.95*

FREEDOM MADE FLESH
The Mission of Christ and His Church

Ignacio Ellacuría

"Ellacuría's main thesis is that God's saving message and revelation are historical, that is, that the proclamation of the gospel message must possess the same historical character that revelation and salvation history do and that, for this reason, it must be carried out in history and in a historical way." *Cross and Crown*

ISBN 0-88344-140-3   *Cloth $8.95*
ISBN 0-88344-141-1   *Paper $4.95*

THE LIBERATION OF THEOLOGY

Juan Luis Segundo

"It is a remarkable book in terms of its boldness in confronting the shortcomings of the Christian tradition and in terms of the clarity of vision provided by the hermeneutic of liberation. Segundo writes with ease whether dealing with the sociological, theological, or political roots of liberation. His is a significant addition to the recent work of Cone, Alves, Moltmann, and Gutiérrez because it compels the movement to interrogate its own theological foundations. A necessary addition, in one of the more fruitful directions of contemporary theology, it is appropriate for graduate, undergraduate, or clerical readers." *Choice*

"The book makes for exciting reading and should not be missing in any theological library." *Library Journal*

ISBN 0-88344-285-X CIP   *Cloth $10.95*
ISBN 0-88344-286-8   *Paper $6.95*

MARX AND THE BIBLE

José Miranda

"An inescapable book which raises more questions than it answers, which will satisfy few of us, but will not let us rest easily again. It is an attempt to utilize the best tradition of Scripture scholarship to understand the text when it is set in a context of human need and misery."

Walter Brueggemann, in Interpretation

ISBN 0-88344-306-6   *Cloth $8.95*
ISBN 0-88344-307-4   *Paper $4.95*

BEING AND THE MESSIAH

The Message of Saint John

José Miranda

"This book could become the catalyst of a new debate on the Fourth Gospel. Johannine scholarship will hotly debate the 'terrifyingly revolutionary thesis that this world of contempt and oppression can be changed into a world of complete selflessness and unrestricted mutual assistance.' Cast in the framework of an analysis of contemporary philosophy, the volume will prove a classic of Latin American theology." *Frederick Herzog, Duke University Divinity School*

ISBN 0-88344-027-X CIP   *Cloth $8.95*
ISBN 0-88344-028-8   *Paper $4.95*

THE GOSPEL IN SOLENTINAME

Ernesto Cardenal

"Upon reading this book, I want to do so many things—burn all my other books which at best seem like hay, soggy with mildew. I now know who (not what) is the church and how to celebrate church in the eucharist. The dialogues are intense, profound, radical. *The Gospel in Solentiname* calls us home."

Carroll Stuhlmueller, National Catholic Reporter

ISBN 0-88344-168-3   *Vol. 1 Cloth $6.95*
ISBN 0-88344-170-5   *Vol. 1 Paper $4.95*
ISBN 0-88344-167-5   *Vol. 2 Cloth $6.95*

THE CHURCH AND POWER IN BRAZIL

Charles Antoine

"This is a book which should serve as a basis of discussion and further study by all who are interested in the relationship of the Church to contemporary governments, and all who believe that the Church has a vital role to play in the quest for social justice." *Worldmission*
ISBN 0-88344-062-8   *Paper $4.95*

HISTORY AND
THE THEOLOGY OF LIBERATION

Enrique Dussel

"The book is easy reading. It is a brilliant study of what may well be or should be the future course of theological methodology."
                                           Religious Media Today
ISBN 0-88344-179-9   *Cloth $8.95*
ISBN 0-88344-180-2   *Paper $4.95*

DOM HELDER CAMARA

José de Broucker

"De Broucker, an internationally recognized journalist, develops a portrait, at once intimate, comprehensive and sympathetic, of the Archbishop of Olinda and Recife, Brazil, whose championship of political and economic justice for the hungry, unorganized masses of his country and all Latin America has aroused world attention."
                                                       America
ISBN 0-88344-099-7   *Cloth $6.95*

THE DESERT IS FERTILE

Dom Helder Camara

"Camara's brief essays and poems are arresting for their simplicity and depth of vision, and are encouraging because of the realistic yet quietly hopeful tone with which they argue for sustained action toward global justice." *Commonweal*
ISBN 0-88344-078-4   *Cloth $3.95*

LOVE AND STRUGGLE IN MAO'S THOUGHT

Raymond L. Whitehead

"Mao's thoughts have forced Whitehead to reassess his own philosophy and to find himself more fully as a Christian. His well documented and meticulously expounded philosophy of Mao's love and struggle-thought might do as much for many a searching reader." *Prairie Messenger*

ISBN 0-88344-289-2 CIP   *Cloth $8.95*
ISBN 0-88344-290-6   *Paper $3.95*

WATERBUFFALO THEOLOGY

Kosuke Koyama

"This book with its vivid metaphors, fresh imagination and creative symbolism is a 'must' for anyone desiring to gain a glimpse into the Asian mind." *Evangelical Missions Quarterly*

ISBN 0-88344-702-9   *Paper $4.95*

ASIAN VOICES IN CHRISTIAN THEOLOGY

Edited by Gerald H. Anderson

"A basic sourcebook for anyone interested in the state of Protestant theology in Asia today. I am aware of no other book in English that treats this matter more completely." *National Catholic Reporter*

ISBN 0-88344-017-2   *Cloth $15.00*
ISBN 0-88344-016-4   *Paper $7.95*

FAREWELL TO INNOCENCE

Allan Boesak

"This is an extremely helpful book. The treatment of the themes of power, liberation, and reconciliation is precise, original, and Biblically-rooted. Dr. Boesak has done much to advance the discussion, and no one who is interested in these matters can afford to ignore his important contribution." *Richard J. Mouw, Calvin College*

ISBN 0-88344-130-6 CIP   *Cloth $4.95*

THE PRAYERS
OF AFRICAN RELIGION

John S. Mbiti

"We owe a debt of gratitude to Mbiti for this excellent anthology which so well illuminates African traditional religious life and illustrates so beautifully man as the one who prays." *Sisters Today*
ISBN 0-88344-394-5 CIP   *Cloth $7.95*

POLYGAMY RECONSIDERED

Eugene Hillman

"This is by all odds the most careful consideration of polygamy and the attitude of Christian Churches toward it which it has been my privilege to see." *Missiology*
ISBN 0-88344-391-0   *Cloth $15.00*
ISBN 0-88344-392-9   *Paper $7.95*

AFRICAN TRADITIONAL RELIGION

E. Bolaji Idowu

"A great work in the field and closely comparable to Mbiti's *African Religions and Philosophy*. It is worthwhile reading." *The Jurist*
ISBN 0-88344-005-9   *Cloth $6.95*

AFRICAN CULTURE
AND THE CHRISTIAN CHURCH

Aylward Shorter

"An introduction to social and pastoral anthropology, written in Africa for the African Christian Churches." *Western Catholic Reporter*
ISBN 0-88344-004-0   *Paper $6.50*

TANZANIA AND NYERERE

William R. Duggan & John R. Civille

"Sympathetic survey of Tanzania's attempt to develop economically on an independent path." *Journal of World Affairs*
ISBN 0-88344-475-5 CIP   *Cloth $10.95*

THE PATRIOT'S BIBLE

Edited by John Eagleson and Philip Scharper

"Following the terms of the Declaration of Independence and the U.S. Constitution, this faithful paperback relates quotes from the Bible and from past and present Americans 'to advance the kingdom and further our unfinished revolution.' " *A.D.*
ISBN 0-88344-377-5   *Paper $3.95*

THE RADICAL BIBLE

Adapted by John Eagleson and Philip Scharper

"I know no book of meditations I could recommend with more confidence to learned and unlearned alike." *St. Anthony Messenger*
ISBN 0-88344-425-9   *Cloth $3.95*
ISBN 0-88344-426-7   *Pocketsize, paper $1.95*

THE LAW AND THE POOR

Frank Parker, S.J.

"This interesting and extraordinarily practical book shows how to make the laws work for the poor rather than against them." *Choice*
ISBN 0-88344-276-0   *Paper $4.95*

DEVELOPMENT: LESSONS FOR THE FUTURE

Thomas Melady and Robert Suhartono

"This volume is written in clear and readable English, with a minimum of professional jargon. It should be of interest to both professionals and interested laymen." *Journal of Economic Literature*
ISBN 0-88344-079-2   *Cloth $6.95*

THE ASSAULT ON AUTHORITY

William W. Meissner

"This is a sober study of authority from a socio-psychological perspective, with strong emphasis on problems of the religious community." *The Critic*
ISBN 0-88344-018-0   *Cloth $7.95*